Introduc

What are the seven tenets? They are the essential fluid and air in which we swim, walk and run in our daily lives. The seven tenets explain why your life is the way it is and how by realizing the Divine Force that surrounds us is a force for love, you can surmount any obstacle and withstand any ill wind.

Not only survive but prosper. For that is why we are here on earth. To learn, to improve, and to gain experiences. To place in the bottom of your heart that love, understanding, caring and serving are the tools we should use to solve every situation.

Sounds easy but in practice it's difficult. Everyday life swirls constantly around us, as if we live in an eye of a hurricane, and every misstep buffets our emotions. Life is a constant hardship for many. We need to rise above the terrain and visualize the road ahead. From the ground it looks rough and rocky, but from on-high the path appears smooth and the destination closer.

God has a set of rules for the road. The set of Divine Laws that he promulgated gives us certainty. We can be sure that our best interests are always in mind. We acknowledge that often the answers to our prayers may take a form that is at first a complete mystery. Eventually we shall learn the supreme logic behind every occurrence.

By realizing who we are, where we are going, the principals that guide us and the meaning of life on this planet, we can step out and see ourselves in a new light. A calm encompassing gentle brightness which surrounds our soul and lets us know that all will be right in the end.

There is a wealth of information about Spiritism, in the five books by the codifier of Spiritism, Allan Kardec, and in the more than four hundred books by Francisco (Chico) C. Xavier, all dictated to him by various spirits. At the bottom of all of the accumulated writing, it is these seven tenets that present to us the context and foundation of our lives.

I've kept you waiting long enough. I am not telling you anything that most of you don't already know. I am only filling in the blanks or more precisely triggering memories of Divine Laws that have been written deep in your conscience.

1. We are Immortal Souls
2. God and Jesus Love Us
3. We have Multiple Lives
4. During our Lives We Pay for Past Debts and Accumulate New Experiences
5. We Live and Learn in Close Family Groups
6. Our Destiny is Mostly Predetermined
7. We are Assisted in our Lives by Unseen Spirit Forces

7 Tenets of Spiritism – How They Impact Your Daily Life

7 Tenets of Spiritism

How They Impact Your Daily Life

By

Brian Foster

http://www.nwspiritism.com/

1st Edition

Table of Contents

Chapter 1 – We are Immortal Souls

Remember when you were in your twenties and you thought you would live forever and appear as you did back then for all eternity. Well, you shall.

While on earth, you will age, become weaker and eventually die. Only your physical covering will return to the elements. Your spirit shall continue.

In spirit form, you look as you think you look. You wear what your thoughts manufacture for you.

How do I know this? Through my own experiences, Near Death Experiences (NDE), and from books that have been delivered to mediums to be recorded, written word by word, by the gentle command of a spirit.

In one of the NDE's I've researched, a woman who accidently overdosed on prescribed medicine talks about being in a waiting room. Full of people who have just died. She begins a conversation with a mid-thirties red-head. A lovely woman, who during their talk gradually became younger looking with a fuller body of shiny red hair. The freckled face beauty didn't realize it, but through the power of her mind she was transforming her appearance to conform to her personal vision of herself.

Personally, I can't wait to lose my stomach, grow back some hair (lose the hair on my ears, if you please) and store away those bags under my eyes. Is that vain of me? Yes it is, I never said I am a perfect Spiritist yet.

Immortality is Longer Than You Think

Did big numbers scare you at school? Like, the age of the earth is 4.54 billion years old. Written out its 4,540,000,000. Take a typical lifespan of 80 years and our normal life is only 0.00000018, or 18 one hundred millionth of the age of the earth.

You will live longer than the earth has been in existence. Think about that. The life you are living now is less than a blink of an eye of your total presence as a spirit, if you only existed for as long as the earth did from birth to the present.

Another way is to think of your total existence is to look at a year, there are 8,760 hours in a year. The lifespan you may live on earth in this incarnation is less than 1/100th of a second.

If I entered the infinity sign into the equation, your current life would recede to almost absolute zero. Which in the face of eternity is the reality of your life on earth at the present.

This is a long explanation for me to get to the point. And that is: what are you worried about! Blink your eyes and click your heels and you will be back in Kansas – or its equivalent.

Of course, all that I have said is utter nonsense. No one places their life in a greater context. We live in the moment. We feel what we feel in the time frame that we know. No matter what I say, or the numbers tell you, the hurt, anger, joy, bewilderment that you pass through every day is important to you.

We still care, we still want, we still have dreams. Dreams that wondrous happenings are just down the road and our life will be transformed.

All I ask is for you to think about the ramifications of immortality. It won't change anything material. It will change your perspective. Not allot, just a little bit. Just enough for you to realize that whatever golden ring you believe you have missed, whatever happiness you so carelessly discarded, or hole you have dug for yourself is not unalterably lost. Only misplaced, to be found once again.

Immortality Impacts the World

If each of us is immortal, then the entire human race is a set of souls that have been placed and withdrawn repeatedly from the chessboard called earth.

The playing pieces are never lost. Only removed temporarily to be used again.

The Divine Intelligence has a plan for each of us and a higher goal for the world in general.

When you think about the injustices and cruelties of this planet, you ask yourself how could this be? It is all part of the plan to improve the collection of souls that inhabit this planet. Remember, no one is truly lost. They may have had to learn a painful lesson for a few brief moments, but they will be set upon the playing field once again when the correct set of factors is ready for their particular needs.

We are all part of this larger picture. I doubt that any of us knows how we are being used to push society and other souls forward.

My friends and I talk and we do see that there is a possibility that helping people find Spiritism is beneficial. But the numbers we reach is relatively small. Although every journey must begin somewhere.

Then we discuss our children also contributing, trying to spy out the big picture. Unfortunately, we look around and see the messy rooms, the unfinished homework and absolutely nothing ever put back in the right place and all hope is temporarily abandoned.

Like grains of sand that accumulate to create a beautiful white sandy beach, each of our small contributions add up. In our own way all of us pull together to move our culture forward. To a time when love and goodness reigns.

Immortality Impacts You

I love the thought of being immortal. My bucket list is eminently doable, now that I realize it's no big deal if I miss some entries in one life. I will have plenty of time to fulfill every desire. I do hope that my wishes mature over the course of my lives and my aspirations become wiser.

When I was young I had dreams of conquest, attaining great wealth or making an impression on the world. As time went on, my wants and plans became more modest. Reality set in and I began to honestly understand my limitations.

I couldn't devote enough time on my passion. The daily grind of gainful employment drained my enthusiasm and strength. At my pace it would take several lifetimes to attain what I wanted.

My passion was history, I wanted to read, write and discuss the great events. I didn't enter college as a history major because I knew there was no money in it. And I sought money. I needed to live as I liked. Unaware that no one lives as they like, not even the richest or most powerful person on the planet.

Life is chock full of compromises. Each new path that we believe will be the true solution degrades into a thousand detours, until the road we thought we were building becomes unrecognizable.

But does it? Is there a long term time-frame that puts our plans into focus and provides the answer?

I had a dream about two years before I started writing about Spiritism. It was one of those extremely vivid dreams where I thought I was awake.

In it, I was talking with a woman. Somehow I felt she was an old girlfriend of mine, but I didn't recognize her. I just had the feeling. A sense that our paths had been intertwined before.

She told me that she had previously offered me a pen two times, but that I didn't pick either one of them up. Which made sense to me, because I had planned to write earlier in my life, but abandoned both attempts.

She looked at me with the expression of a person who is thinking, come on, you know you have done this before, what is your hesitation now. In my mind came the realization that I had written successfully. Authored what and when, I had no clue.

I asked her why she stopped offering me the pens, she replied that I didn't seem interested. At that moment I felt an emptiness within me. But more than that, I was disappointed and yet curious about the future.

I replied, go ahead keep them coming, I might just pick up one someday. She smiled and seem to glow, with the light from her form basking me in a state of contentment.

I had no idea why I had a sense of being totally at ease. It seemed like one of those moments you feel when the answer you have been looking for presents itself. The expression, "something clicked" is a perfect description.

When I awoke, I felt good, as if I when I was a child I had just drank a hot cocoa. As the day passed my contentment faded away. Within a week I had left behind the dream. It was no longer on my agenda.

About a year later, I had an urge to write an article. I had read *The Spirits Book* and the other four books by Allan Kardec. So I moved to a book by Francisco C. Xavier, also known as Chico to all of Brazil.

Francisco "Chico" Xavier

Chico was voted the greatest Brazilian of the twentieth century. No medium has approached his stature. The spirit realm never gave him an easy or luxurious time. To begin with, Chico had a hard childhood.

At the age of five, his mother died. Unable to care alone for his nine children, Chico's father split the children up amongst various friends and family. Chico went to his godmother, who was an extremely cruel person. She spanked and tortured Chico. She would stab him with a fork in his stomach and not let him pull it out.[1] He only gained solace during these times by speaking with the spirit of his dead mother.

Thankfully, his father remarried, to a wonderful woman, Cidália Batista, who agreed to marry only if he would reunite all of his children. From then until the time of her death, when Chico was seventeen, Chico possessed his greatest support among the living. He had to work at an early age supporting his large extended family. Finally in 1924, while working, he finished primary school, afterwards he never went back.[2] In 1927, his step-mother passed away, in May of the same year, the spirit of his mother directed to him to read Allan Kardec's *The Spirits Book.*

Chico was attacked by many as being one of a large legion of imposters, whose only aim was to increase his personal wealth. Chico said that he could never fall down, since he never stood up, meaning that he couldn't be charged as a money seeking person because he never took money. All proceeds from his books were donated to charity.

The range of books written by Chico was enormous. From books by deceased poets, suicides, a young man describing learning at a school in heaven, to books by Emmanuel, which consisted of his past lives and the past lives of people he knew while he was on earth. Including, Emmanuel's first encounter with Jesus Christ, in which he completely rejected Jesus.

Chico was the first person to tell the world, that he never wrote anything, he only wrote what was communicated to him by the spirit realm. He wrote a total of 469 books before he died, on June 30, 2002.

Emmanuel was Chico's spirit mentor. He was constantly at Chico's side. From the spirit world he managed the other spirit authors who wish to write books and the legions of spirits who merely wished to send short messages to loved ones still on earth.

Emmanuel, in one of his past lives was the Roman senator Publius Lentulus, who was present in the holy land during the time of Jesus. Just to dissuade you that everyone with past lives are always born noble and glorious, in his next life Emmanuel was born a slave who was fated to die in the Roman circus as one of the Christians doomed to die for their belief.

Originally, Emmanuel give Chico a goal of thirty books. A

Spiritist who worked with Chico, Geraldo, gave a lecture about his time working with Chico, he tells that when Chico finished his quota of thirty books, his spirit mentor Emmanuel told Chico, "Now that you have finished thirty books, how about doubling that to get to a goal of sixty books?"

"No problem", replied Chico. Then when Chico reached that goal, Emmanuel asked, "Why not go to one hundred books?"

Again, Chico said, "No problem."

Chico reached his one hundredth book around the time when he was sixty. He wanted to retire, however, his spirit guide, Emmanuel, told him that he had bad news for Chico, Jesus had decreed that Chico will spend the rest of his life writing more books. Chico liked to tease and responded, "Well, we have freewill, don't we?"

"Of course you have freewill, you can choose not to write more books." replied Emmanuel.

"Then, I don't wish to write more books." Chico responded.

Emmanuel then told Chico, "In that case I have a second decree from Jesus, if you don't wish to write more books, then your life will end tomorrow."

Chico laughed and said, "No, no, no, I will write more books."[3]

Back to my Pen Dream

The book that I read was a book psychographed by Chico, under the inspiration of Emmanuel. The name of the book is, *On the Way to the Light*, which details how the spirit world has guided the destiny of the earth.

The contents were a revelation to me, it put in place the individual quest, through successive incarnations, to become a better soul within the broader picture of moving the earth forward. Toward a goal of becoming a just and fair society.

Reading the book was like watching an old fashion epic.

Scenes of the evolution of generations unfolded, what appeared to be random events coalesced into meaningful progress over spans of hundreds of years.

Suddenly the veil was lifted, our small little steps to learn through each life was part of a gradual march for the entire planet. All orchestrated by the Supreme Intelligence.

I was possessed by an undeniable urge to put thoughts to paper. Then I remembered my dream. I picked-up the pen. Finally, I intuitively understood what I was required to do.

Could I have possessed the necessary skills to communicate Spiritism to the English speaking world without prior training? I think not.

I just realized the prior paragraph sounds pretentious, it's not meant to be. Maybe, I should write, communicate Spiritism to those few who are interested and wish to comprehend why their lives have followed a certain path.

I believe I was carefully guided from life to life to enable me to attain the required set of skills to fulfill a part of my life's plan.

Immortality enables intricate threads, which get lost within the entire tapestry, but are nevertheless present providing structure for the future.

What we endure in this life, just might be setting us up for something marvelous in the next. It's the same as going to college and learning a subject, but having no idea who you are going to work for and how exactly will you apply your knowledge.

The horrible experiences you encounter may actually prepare you for a position of great responsibility in the next life much more than an easy calm life could provide you with the required training.

If you are able, step back from your trials and analyze what has taught you the most. Was it sitting on a chaise lounge with a drink by the pool or digging yourself out of a financial hole? Yes, you certainly deserve the good times, but realize the difficult periods in your life are setting you up for a greater challenge. A more fulfilling episode in a future life.

Learn to fly to the fifty thousand foot level and view the road you have taken in all of its grandeur. You have learned more than you think, you have endured better than you give yourself credit for. Be proud that you are still making progress and don't be worried that you aren't as rich or successful as you want to be, because, frankly, those are just temporary merit badges. What you have is your mind and experiences, the only allowable baggage to take with you after your physical death.

Immortality Impacts Others

Once you start seeing your own life, the life of others around you begin to make sense. Their seemingly random pursuits and decisions, based on who knows what criteria, become patterns.

You start to detect themes and notice flaws that beg to be corrected. Beware, remember what Jesus said about noticing the speck in your neighbor's eye while have you a plank in yours.

I have a friend, who unerringly selects the wrong woman to enter into a relationship. While he is caring and would do anything for a woman, treat her like the proverbial princess, he selects those who see it as a sign of weakness.

I ask myself, I who am perfect, how could he continually make such a mistake. There are a multitude of gracious caring woman who would appreciate a kind soul.

What is worse, he stays with these woman even as they treat him in a downward spiral of take, take and more take without any giving on their part. He is like red meat to a tiger.

One could put on their Freudian hat and announce he must like being treated like a doormat. This could be true, but why is the question. Again, modern psychoanalysis would proclaim it's from his childhood. Again, could be true.

There is another answer and it is rooted in past lives. As an immortal soul my friend, is learning the lessons of what he probably did wrong in a past life. My conjecture, is that he was on the other side of the equation and now must experience what it is like to be treated as he treated others.

All one can do is to sympathize and show support, wherever and whenever one can. My friend is in the middle of a tough but lasting lesson. He shall emerge stronger and more capable in the next life.

We all have friends who are in the midst of struggles which re-occur. Love them and support them, do not expect a miracle or a light to turn on. It may happen, but recognize that the spirit realm has planned a remedy for past mistakes. The future will be bright, your friends will conquer their deficiencies.

Immortality means that nothing is final. At any age your dreams, hopes and aspirations may still come true. If not in this life, then in the next or the next or in the spirit world.

You are immortal. Your spirit will live forever. You will experience life after life in a quest to perfect yourself. You have a mission, the most important mission possible; to improve, to love, to be charitable. To be part of a grand plan to not only raise yourself, but your neighbors and the entire human race to where the earth will truly be a paradise.

Chapter 2 – God and Jesus Loves Us

"You have no idea how much love the spirit world has for you", is my paraphrased version of what the most celebrated medium of 20th century Brazil, Francisco (Chico) Xavier, told us near the end of his life. Chico loved the people of Brazil so much he asked his spiritual mentors the right to die only when the people of Brazil would not excessively grieve. The answer to his prayer was that he passed away days after Brazil won the 2002 World Cup, in the midst of a national celebration.

I went through most of my life absolutely ignorant that I am loved by any other entity besides my parents. I was always surprised that even they loved me. I felt grateful that since they were my parents they had no choice in the matter. It came with the territory.

Growing up, I was busy being me. I was self-satisfied, smarter than anyone else and generally unfeeling toward others. I had, at the very least, the self-awareness that I wasn't a kind, cuddly, caring sort of person. Whenever the opposite sex found me attractive and demonstrated their interest I was somewhat amused. Obviously, they didn't know the real isolated me.

I did have a moral code. I believed in honor, although I violated it many times. I rationalized away my principles in the quest for a momentary gain or just a sense of temporary peace. I was like many others, not a particularly harmful member of society, but not a force for good either. I merely worked and paid my share of taxes.

Even in the midst of all of my unattractiveness, I was looked on from afar by kind seeing eyes. I can visualize them now, shaking their heads at another dumb move I was in the middle of contemplating. After each incident they would hope against all expectations that someday I would learn the basic lessons and be civilized.

Until I too had children I couldn't understand the depth of love that one could have for a defenseless creature. It helps that with their big heads and fat little bodies they are very cute. With us older grimier adults I don't see the attraction. Nevertheless, through their own experiences, spirits empathize with our plight. They have walked in our shoes, possessed the same misconceptions, and placed material goods over people and all other follies I have committed and then some.

What Kind of Love

There are many types of love, from the big sister or brother for their siblings, parent for child, aunt or uncle for their nieces and nephews to the all-out passionate love for another. The range is enormous. So, when we hear God is Love what does that mean?

Love comes in many flavors, do we just get one? Or, are we loved in different ways? How exactly does God, Jesus and the spirit world loves us? It's important to know.

Why is it vital to understand this point? After all, isn't love good enough? Knowing that we are loved and not hated and not being used as playthings in some sort of massive inter-galactic video game, isn't that good enough for us? The answer is no, not really. Because, we humans being fallible, constantly judge the amount of love we receive and use any change to moderate the love we return.

We do this first with parents. When I was young and got into trouble, I would get mad, not at myself, of course! At my parents! My mother would tell stories that I would fling everything out of my room in a show of self-sufficiency and defiance. I didn't need them. No sir, not one little bit.

If that didn't do the trick, I would pack up my little lunch box and leave for parts unknown; never to return. After the cookies ran out, about a half of block or so, I would come to my senses and return.

Are we any different as adults? We reject our loved one at the first sign of discord. Unless the road is smooth as glass and we are constantly happy we stay committed. But, God forbid, at the first sign of a pothole or a patch of gravel we eject immediately.

Feeling sorry for yourself because others don't love you as they should is a full-time job. It saps our energy and our attitude. Worse, it deflects us from our prime objective; to become better, to increase our capacity for love.

Therefore, we need to recognize that the rough spots aren't arrows of hate or indifference from the spirit world. Often, the harder we have it, the more we are loved.

What do I mean by this? Let's begin by examining the different types of love, according to me, since I want to keep this short and not write a book about every nook and cranny of the varieties of love.

Basically, there are four types of love, with many shades in-between. Let's start with the first type we experience as we enter the world. Little bundles who cry, gas, make diapers dirty and wake up whenever we darn well feel like it. Never a moment of regret passes our minds, since we only want what we want exactly when we want it.

Parental Love

Love from your parents is wonderful and awful at different times. When you are young the feeling you have with your mother or father during those times of peace or of needed reassurance supplies you the energy to go out and survive the world.

I remember feelings of anxiety about bullies in the class. I would talk to my dad. He would tell me of the necessity of not inviting conflict but also being prepared. He told me that you must stand up for yourself, because there are many times no one else will. He spent the weekend showing me how to defend myself. Me, with my little fists, hesitantly lashing out, making no impact whatsoever on my fit father. Little by little, by repetition, I gained confidence and ability.

On Monday, the event was anti-climactic. I merely stood and

stared at my adversaries. It was as if they could read my mind. I wasn't scared, I was ready. Off they went to pester the next poor child.

God has put us on this earth for the same reason. He loves us and he knows that we must make our way in an imperfect world. We aren't just deposited on terra firma with no tools to survive. We are carefully guided, with parents who fit the trials in we requested or require, with the family and friends who have been sent along with us to facilitate our journey.

We talk about unconditional love and how we should be loved in any condition, which is true, but too often the meaning morphs into unconditional luxury of living. As if the Divine Power owes us a strife free life. Is that love? Not preparing your children for real life is the antithesis of love, it is dereliction of duty.

God loves us and as a consequence we are forced into uncomfortable situations. Trials where, if given our druthers, we would never sign up for, nevertheless an intelligence far greater than ours has determine it is just the thing we need.

We see examples of this every day. There is the story of a woman who was not happy with her life and prayed to God to help her find happiness, even though she had a successful career and a good husband. She even considered him a perfect husband. Much better than all of her friend's spouses. Still, she wasn't satisfied with her life, she wanted more.

Then she was in a bad accident and sustained a severe back injury. She was on constant pain medication and couldn't function. Her career was in shambles.

Then did she determine to try once more to ask God for help. She yelled at God demanding that she be saved. She blamed God for her troubles. Not only did God not make her happy but ruined her life.

After demanding assistance from God, she and her husband went to a restaurant and as she approached she felt immense energy all about her. A large presence loomed that heightened her senses and caused her to look in every direction.

At the restaurant, she drank excessively. Her husband managed to get her to the car, she threw-up on the drive home, next she attempted to walk to the house after they arrived. Whereupon she fell down and hit her head on the sidewalk. Her worried husband took her to the hospital.

Suddenly she notices a calmness, she seemed to float in a sea of tranquility. The hospital staff and even strangers approached her, wanting to talk. This had never happened to her before.

Her husband looked on incredulous. This was a different wife than he was used to.

She started to feel the thoughts and feelings radiating from others. Her mind became a beacon of energy, sending thoughts and receiving them, becoming more in tune to the stream of feelings from others.

She felt her body completely morph into a sensing organism. Her senses extended deep into her body. She felt complete comfort. She knew wonderful events were about to happen.

She is now a practicing medium, helping others solve the problems in their lives.

God answered her prayers. She became happy and newly in love with her husband, but only after great suffering. And, what she thought at the time of her second prayer to God, the complete destruction of everything she had striven to attain. A good career, money to spend and save, all gone. She desperately wanted it all back.

Yet, the Supreme Intelligence knew that in order for her to really find happiness, her whole life had to be radically changed. She journeyed through immense pain and suffering. In the end, she emerged a better person.

In essence, one aspect of love from God is we get what we

need, not what we desire. Sounds a little like tough love doesn't it? That's the awful part of parental love, at least for the child in us, we don't get what we want; we get what is good for us.

The Supreme Intelligence in the universe is wise to our tricks and empty promises. We are looked upon like children swearing to take care of their pet forever.

A friend of mine loves to tell the story where his daughter wanted a hamster so bad, she took a solemn oath to eternally care for the furry animal. Well, the first two weeks, the maintenance was awesome. Within a couple of months the hamster had starved to death. When his daughter found the animal dead, she convulsed in tears and set up an elaborate funeral. My friend had to stop himself from blurting out, "But you killed it! Why are you crying now?"

Imagine the spirit world watching us whine and struggle through well-place obstacles, thinking the same thing, "You asked for it, why are you whining now!" Because, we are now placed in a human body and our ability to connect cause and effect is often broken by a thousand distractions.

How many times have you sat back and really thought about why an event occurred? I confess, almost never. I just react and throw my hands in the air with disgust. Why did that girlfriend in college never want to go out again after a few dates? At the time I just thought, that's her problem and moved on. But, if I took the time and reflected on the reasons, such as calling her back when I felt like it or being my usual sarcastic self, then I might have learned a lesson. I may have, God forbid, actually improved at an earlier age.

If I could manage to survive through my teenage (and early twenties) years and learn to listen to the accumulated wisdom of my parents, there is no reason why I can't do the same with Jesus.

Instead of reacting, I need to stay on an even keel and reflect. Review the good and look at the bad experiences as opportunities to excel. God, Jesus and the spirit world have all worked together to create a plan, a plan with my benefit in mind, the least I can do is to realize the plan wasn't created with malice but with love.

The Love of a Mentor

We soon realize how invaluable it is to have a mentor. A mentor is a person who looks at you as your own individual, with potential which should be guided and encouraged. This could be your uncle or aunt when you are younger or more often a business colleague who perceives a quality about you that others have not.

This is the most unselfish love of all. Helping because at some point, in the distant future, you will be able to add value to society and assist others. No reciprocation is expected, the mentor is usually paying forward what another has done for her or him.

I had one like that as I first started working. He was a wonderful and intelligent man who originally came from Ethiopia looking for a better life. I remember asking him about the Italian occupation before World War II and thinking he would tell me of the atrocities and the cruel imposition of the colonial power. He told me that the Italians were the only ones who ever did anything good for his country.

They built roads and schools and generally attempted to treat everyone with justice. Unlike the Ethiopian Emperor Haile Selassie, who considered the country to be his own piggy bank with no need to care for the people. After the Italians were forced to withdraw at the end of the conflict, everything went back to chaos and injustice, once again, became the norm.

I marveled at his absence of emotion and his level headed analysis of the situation. He recognized the benefits and the pitfalls and tried to weigh them without prejudice. He possessed an unerring sense of rightness.

I never heard him trying to scheme others out of what was theirs or try and cut moral corners. Not that the world was black and white, but one should strive to find the right balance and be honorable in your dealings.

We both worked for a person who was none of that. We tried to refashion the work as best we could to insure everyone benefited. Once I was asked and I foolishly agreed to personally sign a lease for a piece of equipment on the day my mentor was away on business.

Looking back on it, I now realize the timing was deliberate. My naiveté was just too inviting. When my friend returned, he looked at me and said that, well, the lesson will be valuable for you and shouldn't be too expensive down the road. Of course he was correct. I was stuck paying off the lease long after the employment vanished.

Not that I learned my lesson, afterwards I tried to start my own business and failed, disappointing people and losing their money. Worse, I didn't handle the defeat with dignity and ownership, but blamed the world around me. My fault was that I rationalized away the lessons my mentor gave to me. I tried to cut corners to survive. Whereas, I should have maintained a code of ethics and failed with grace. I never put myself in that type of situation again.

Sometimes it takes years and practice for the lesson to really sink in. It's the same with how the spirit world guides us. They are very patient, they have to be when they have a hard-headed student like me.

Love that Makes You Feel Good

Let me put it out there right away, doing good makes you feel good. Studies have shown this to be a truism. Helping others is the surest way to help yourself out of whatever emotional hole has swallowed you.

Imagine having a job where you get paid for providing care for those you love. A career where you work with others who toil with the same dedication. No politics, no office gossip, no cliques to distract from the job at hand. These are the conditions in which good spirits perform their duties.

Spirits are all around us, supplying assistance, care and love.

They send out radiating thoughts of sympathy that we absorb. We may not realize it, but when you wake up refreshed, or just when your mood changes for no apparent reason, the catalyst is the field of love from the guardian spirits who surround us.

I take advantage of this. When I am tired of working and am on the verge of whining about my pathetic circumstances. I try and remember to sit back and meditate on the help I am receiving. Unless, I engage in stubborn self-pity, I usually emerge with renewed strength and confidence.

Of course this is a cyclical occurrence. I frequently forget to meditate first and go directly to whining. One would think my spirit mentors would say to themselves, when is this guy going to take responsibility and pull himself up and out of his black hole. Maybe I should think about it.

Love that Transports You to Ecstasy

There are three types in this category. First, the fresh breath of a new love, where you can hardly think straight and your emotions are highly charged. Great feeling, but this love, while part of a Divine attribute, is not the direct light of God's love.

Second, the excitement of sex: let me digress a bit about this type of love. I read an interesting view from a book inspired by the spirit Andre Luiz, on why we do have sex on earth. And surprise it's not just there to make us feel good.

The Reason for Sex

> "The control center of sex is not located in the dense body, but in the sublime organization of the soul"[4]

I read this in one of Francisco (Chico) C. Xavier's books, *In the Greater World*, and was intrigued. If there was anything about us that seemed to be rooted in our dense primitive and often brutish bodies it is sex!

The spirit that dictated the book to Chico Xavier, Andre Luiz, who by the way, wrote thirteen books, all from the spirit world. All exposing what is life like after we leave our physical bodies.

In Andre Luiz's books, he is usually part of a team of spirits who are sent to help us on earth. Andre learns valuable information from his team leaders. In this book Andre Luiz's mentor tell us what sex means in the higher spiritual regions and how it molds us here on earth.

> "Down on earth, men and women are distinguished according to specific organic features. As for us, in transit to higher spiritual regions, the remembrance of our earthly existence is still preponderant. We know, however, that in such higher regions femininity and masculinity are characteristics of souls that are highly passive or openly active."[5]

To the spirit world sex is an attitude, or more succinctly an attribute. Attributes that we acquire throughout our many lives. He describes this process further:

> "Consequently, we know that, in the variations of our experiences, we gradually acquire divine qualities such as determination and tenderness, strength and humility, power and gentleness, intelligence and sentiment, initiative and intuition, wisdom and love, until we attain our supreme balance in God."[6]

As we progress we learn to balance the active and passive sides of our nature. Every spirit is unique and all will have different degrees, but all who ascend into purity will achieve a balance.

Andre's mentor tells us that the human race started out like animals, where the male possessed the female, but given millennia of slow evolution the combinations of woman-mother and man-father migrated to the concept of the tribe, the primitive shelter changed into the home and the quest for wild game transformed into the farm. From this, the spark of sex, civilization arose, the wooden club of the caveman became the gift of flowers to his love.

We all must travel this road to prefect balance. The mentor describes our journey:

> "Sometimes, humans take years, centuries and many lifetimes

to go from one level to the next. Few individuals are able to keep themselves above the fray with the equilibrium that is required. Very few have crossed the territory of ownership without battling cruelly with the monsters of selfishness and jealousy, to which they have completely surrendered. A small number travel the road of tenderness without shackling themselves for a long stretch to the many chains of exclusiveness. And sometimes, only after millennia of excruciating, purifying trials, can the soul reach the luminous zenith of sacrifice for it final deliverance in route to new cycles of unification with the Divinity."[7]

Therefore, we own no one, we direct no one, we merely love, cherish and help one another. Always providing feedback for the spiritual benefit of our partner. Each one of us learning to weigh our active and passive sides. Learning to know when one is better than the other in different circumstances.

So be warned, the debate about how men are becoming like women and women becoming like men is actually just starting. As we mature as souls we all shall have a mixture, a perfect blend of caring and action.

As for me, I am far from it, my ability to quietly empathize and not give direct solutions to even the most veiled problems is completely lacking. But this doesn't stop me from trying!

Love Driving You to Ecstasy

There is a third moment in our lives when we do feel fully enveloped in love. Sometimes a child feels it when close to her or his mother. For adults, it may never happen again. But when it does, it is a memorable event.

I have only experienced it twice in my lifetime. The feeling is hard to describe, and it may be different for each person. For me, it was like an electrical pulse throughout my entire body, a feeling of lightness. I could sense an affinity with all things. I have never felt so at ease, so calm and at peace. I hate to say it, but here goes, it was even better than sex!

How did I reach that level? First, I never even felt close to basking in real love until I began to explore Spiritism. I thought I did, but when I felt the impact of Divine Love, I knew that my previous standard was set very low.

About a year after I began reading Allan Kardec's and some of Chico Xavier's book, I realized that I needed to reshape not just my attitude and outward personality, but my thoughts as well. I needed to be more caring and loving.

Soon after I had a dream. It was a short, yet extremely powerful dream. My mother was holding me and for the first time I knew in my heart I was allowed to feel, for just a few seconds, the power of Divine love.

Another year passed and my wife and I created our Spiritist group. There was a woman who was part of the group. She talked about a person she had met on the internet. A woman of little means who was gravely ill and didn't have the resources to find help. The woman lived in a rural area of France.

I remember sitting there listening to the member of our little circle speak about how she knew she didn't have the money to help, since she too, had little. But, in spite of it all she would continue to look for ways to assist.

Slowly, I could feel my arms tingling and my entire body reacting to the scene of two women, neither possessing the wherewithal to effectively change their lives, but in spite of their lack of material goods, they continued to strive. At that moment I felt, for the second time, a wave of love immersing me.

I have heard others talk about a similar sensation when experiencing a highly religious moment. But the most consistent trigger that I have detected is for people who have had Near Death Experiences.

When they are not in this world but the spirit realm, they speak of the glorious comfort of being bathed in joy and love. An emotional wave so potent that they beg not to be returned to the physical world. Only the sorrow of leaving loved ones was enough to convince them to return.

This lightness of being, happiness to the highest power, all-encompassing compassion for every creature is our goal.

Not just a wish, like a discarded New Year's Resolution, but a goal that is given to every soul by God. For all of us are to one day achieve the status of being a pure spirit.

This is on everyone's dance card and can't be erased or crossed-out. The speed at which we reach our target is entirely up to us.

Chapter 3 – We Have Multiple Lives

Before I discovered Spiritism, I would play a mind game. I would die in a tragic accident. A complete innocent, my life cut short by the fault of another. I would appear at the pearly gates.

Saint Peter would be there. I hoped that seeing me, in my pristine victimhood, Saint Peter would welcome me to heaven with open arms.

But my mind wouldn't let me finish my daydream so nicely. I would show up, in front of the gatekeeper and he would say, "Well, Brian, you're here, why do you think you should get in."

I would look downcast and answer, "I died in a terrible accident."

Saint Peter would have that look that teachers do, when they know a student is telling them anything but the correct answer, because they don't have a clue what it is. If only they could keep talking, somehow they would stumble upon the right sequence of words, "Yes, but what have you done to deserve to go to heaven?"

"I have tried to be good."

Saint Peter was very smart and gave me a stinging retort, "First of all, you didn't really believe in the concept of heaven or that God was all that interested in you, did you?"

I had an answer for that," But I do now, I can see the pearly gates." I added for effect, "And I never had the chance to get in the habit of expressing my loving caring side."

Saint Peter would then ask, "And when were you planning for that to happen?"

After that, I would shut off my mind game, because this was going nowhere fast. I like to win and I didn't see a way out of that conversation. Except a real course of action, which I knew I would rationalize away at the first opportunity.

Now that I know we have multiple lives, I should feel satisfaction that in this life I began by being at worst intellectually lazy and a believer in pleasure over work.

After all, when we were primitive spirits, we took what we want and left the moralizing to others. Such was the state of the earth thousands of years ago and still the case in too many locations today.

The simple fact that at the minimum I had become semi-civilized was at least a small victory. But then I was presented with Spiritism and I dove in head first.

For the first time I received concrete answers to my larger questions. Such as, why are we here? Who is God? What is God? Why is the earth simultaneously a beautiful and a terrible place?

Reading the answers in Allan Kardec's *The Spirits Book* was riveting. No wonder people like Thomas Edison and Sir Arthur Conan Doyle were believers.

The answers felt right, they fit the puzzle in my mind perfectly. I believed because of what I read and what I experienced. In no other manner could I explain how events were foretold to me came true with uncanny accuracy.

Others had experienced the same thing. For the first time I wasn't incredulous at their statements. But could I believe all that I read or was the Doctrine wrong in areas? Did we really live multiple lives?

Most would tell me that I had to have faith. To me faith is a funny object. I have it, but not really. I could never move a mountain with my faith. I needed proof, not absolute concrete evidence, merely enough to construct a logical foundation.

This is where Spiritism is unique. Spiritism doesn't believe in miracles. All can be explained by understanding the Divine Laws. What we see as miracles have an explanation that we are to backwards to comprehend.

Spiritism foretells of the day when Science, Philosophy and Religion merge and work with each other to promote a complete view of the physical and spiritual world.

Faith is wonderful to possess, but it should be anchored by reasoning. The first step toward understanding came during a trip to Rio de Janeiro, it was in winter, but nicer than summers in Seattle. I was given a hint of my previous lives.

My wife and I attended a mediums meeting. I am not a medium, I have no aptitude in that regard. I was a spectator. During the meeting I notice one of the mediums at the table writing down a message.

After the meeting concluded, it was announced there was a message for my wife and I. I will not go into detail since it was meant to be just for us.

However, I will reveal what we were told about our past lives. That the both of us had been married before and that we had sought after power and treasure at the expense of our moral code.

Furthermore, we had failed people who had been under our tutelage. And this is the sad part, not once but again and again.

It hurts to even write these words. Knowing that I betrayed the trust of those with whom I should protect.

After that message the reason for my career path became apparent. I had started out as a programmer after college, but being ambitious I rose to become a manager, then at the director and vice-president level.

As I ascended, I had a progressively harder time following the corporate line to squeeze employees out of their last drop of productivity and then abandon them without looking back.

I couldn't follow the modern corporate attitude that everything was a question of profit and that a sense of honor was unimportant. Not to say I didn't try my hardest to be a ruthless person. I failed again, many times.

I soon realized I couldn't lie effectively to the workers around me and I had no taste for the constant political intrigue. It was repugnant to me.

Finally I decided to go back to the ranks and manage projects, not people.

It was my collective failures in past lives that had molded me to reject my ambitious behavior. While living I had seen, and most probably in other lives been on the receiving end of my types of wrongs, to place deep into my conscience to not do this another time.

For quite a while I rationalized away the stirrings of my inside voice, but eventually, thank God, I turned away and became one of the little unnoticed minions. Expendable at any moment. Materially poorer but spiritually reinforced. A trade I shall take at any time.

Reincarnation from Three Religions

Various religions recognize the need for multiple lives. The chance that anyone of us could become entirely a force for good in one life is next to nil.

Why would a loving God let some be born into completely dire circumstances, into families where a life of crime is obligatory? How could anyone expect a normal soul to rise above that to perfection in one life? Whereas, we like to believe all can become good, we realize deep into our hearts that adverse environments could make the transition almost impossible.

I found this marvelous book, *Jesus, Buddha, Krishna & Lao Tzu*, by Richard Hooper. In it he compares similar passages in different combinations of four religious prophets.

Many scholars analyze who was first to create the moral tenets and who stole what idea from whom. Whereas, Spiritist realize there are many similarities because they were sent to earth to preach the same doctrine. Each slightly affected by different cultures and times.

Here is what Richard Hopper gathered about reincarnation from three different religions:

> Jesus: Be merciful that you may obtain mercy. Forgive, so that you may be forgiven. As you judge, so you will be judged. As you serve, so will service be done to you. And whatever you measure out, that is what will be returned to you. [The Gospel According to Matthew]
>
> Krishna: Everyone creates their own fate. Even life in the womb is affected by the karma from a previous life. [The Garuda Purana]
>
> Buddha: From a sound, an echo returns. A body creates a shadow. So, too, will misery come to him who does evil works. [Three Sermons][8]

All three could have been lifted from the Doctrine of Spiritism. Our actions in one life shall affect our next life. How much plainer could all three be?

When Jesus says what is measured out will be returned to you, how can that be true without the concept of multiple lives? We all know or have heard of dishonest people who have gotten away with many crimes.

Yes there is a type of purgatory, where one stays only as long as one rejects the path of love and fraternity. Then the poor spirit is taken to be helped in one of the many celestial waystations to enable wounded souls to repair and find the light.

Spiritism tells us that to improve as spirits we must spend our time in the physical world. No other atmosphere is as effective at forcing us to mend our ways.

The combination of our physical bodies and the onslaught of emotions which come with our temporary material space suit serve to focus with bright intensity the lessons we require. The results are seared into our minds and hearts.

Why then do people still insist on committing wrong deeds?

Because, many do not believe that we truly are spirit beings who come to earth to learn and pay our debts. I can certainly understand that. I was in that category for many years. But once you internalize the enormity of reincarnation, your entire outlook alters and sacrificing the progress of your soul for momentary material gain becomes out of the question.

We should realize the benefits of committing good deeds. Spiritism tells us that every sacrifice, every soul we assist in their trials will be paid back a hundredfold. We know this, why else when happiness is measured, the first on the list is the joy we get in helping others.

I read in Spiritist literature where giving your time and effort, putting others first and denying yourself in the meantime is like pruning a tree. You will grow stronger, your faith and love will shine more brightly. People will be attracted to your aura.

Case in Point

A famous Portuguese author, known as the Portuguese Balzac, wrote many books and plays at the end of the nineteenth century. His name was Camilo Castelo Blanco. Look him up, there is a Wikipedia site dedicated to him.

As he became older, two tragedies afflicted him, first his son committed suicide and second he was going blind due to the ravages of syphilis.

Camilo had no wish to continue on blind and bereft of family in his old age. He took the easy way out and chose death.

For all intents and purposes that should have been the end of the story. A small Wikipedia entry and books that would gather dust in a musky old bookshop or forgotten in attics.

It wasn't the end of the story. It was the beginning. Camilo brought to the world the arc of his life, through the medium Yvonne A. Pereira to write his life after physical death biography.

In the book, *Memoirs of a Suicide*, we are taken from the

moment Camilo kills himself to years later to when he is preparing to re-enter our physical world to subject himself to the required trials to pay for his wrongs and to learn the lessons so he may improve his immortal spirit.

As part of his therapy, provided by "Mary of Nazareth" Hospital. A spirit colony reserved for suicides, men and women, to recuperate after their ordeal and to learn about their sacred mission to fully live out the life they had chosen beforehand.

Running in cowardice from your assigned tribulations in your physical life, results in severe penalties. As part of his rehabilitation, Camilo must learn what brought him to his decision to escape his ailments and why he was given the sufferings that he should have endured with dignity.

To understand how he arrived at the decision he made at that particular point in time, he was shown, as if in a 3D movie, his previous lives.

The first life he was shown was at the time of Christ, Camilo witnessed that he was "a wretched person, poor and evil."[9] He lived off of the discarded clothes and food of others. His greatest pleasure was to witness misfortune, of any kind, drunks, fights and torture. He finds himself following Jesus, so he can witness pain and suffering:

> "Fierce in my obstinacy, I follow him on his dolorous climb, yelling offenses and vile scorn; and I must confess that the only reason I do not strike him with stones with the violence of my murderous arm is because he is so closely guarded by the Roman soldiers. The truth is that I have always felt myself to be inferior and belittled everywhere I go. I feel envy and hatred towards everything that actually is, or that I believe to be, superior to me! Ugly, disheveled, ignoble, deformed – I had only one arm – degraded, ambitious, the stuff of pure evil dripped from my heart."[10]

Wait, it gets worse. He notices Mary, the mother of Jesus, and yells out insults and sarcastic remarks to her. Anything to hurt everyone around him. A man with one arm, for what offense he lost an arm, we will never know, but he was on a mission to equally harm the world. A man who was rescued from the valley of the suicides by the very woman he abused more than 1800 years earlier.

I can't imagine the nightmare of discovering his deeds. I can only contemplate in fear what horrible crimes I must have committed in some previous wretched life. For all of us are on the path to become better, which means that in the past we have been that which we scorn and disapprove of today.

Camilo then was shown his next life. He was born into an impoverished noble family, in 17th century Spain. Through his intellectual gifts he enlisted a parish priest to educate him.

Camilo loved a local woman, who in turn loved and married a better prospect. His bitterness enveloped him. He wanted revenge. But first he had to become successful.

He decided to enter the priesthood. The spirit world tried to stop him from this decision. They sent him dreams night after night that he should stay where we was and find a local woman to marry.

Unfortunately, as he was in his previous life he persisted in his present life and let his baser emotions control his actions. He ignored the warnings and joined the Jesuits.

This was at the time of the Spanish Inquisition. A black mark on the Catholic Church. Given his willingness to be cruel, he rose quickly in the hierarchy.

Until one day he spotted the woman who spurned him. He vowed to take revenge. He manipulated events where he went to visit often the family he was targeting.

Camilo attempted to seduce her. She rejected his advances. Even her husband knew of his intentions, but the threat of the Inquisition was so great, he could do nothing.

Finally, seeing he was unsuccessful, Camilo arranged her

husband to be arrested and tortured. Only then, did she agree to sleep with him.

After a time, he grew tired of her reluctance and agreed to release her husband. He had one more surprise for her. Instead of simply letting her husband leave his cell, Camilo had him blinded first.

Now Camilo knew why he was fated to go blind in his next life. It was Supreme Justice. His task was to suffer through the same blindness that he had inflicted upon another.

Camilo now realized he would have to return to a physical body to completely internalize the lessons he was required to learn. He was told the good spirits of the "Mary of Nazareth Hospital", would assist him in his next life. Providing the guidance to keep him on the path to enlightenment.

The spirit world does not want us to fail. We are watched with the loving kindness of a true mother and father. Their affection rains down upon us. This is why we have a conscience. Whereas, we don't retain our memories from past lives when we are reborn, we do have two vital signal posts.

The first is our conscience; our accumulated moral learning from all of our past lives serves to govern us in our daily decisions. When we reflect on an action, our conscience provides us feedback; we must listen to that advice and heed it. For within us we have centuries of stored wisdom.

Our instincts are the second guide rail that has been betrothed to us in our current life. Multiple life experiences in countless sets of circumstances have toned our instincts, whereby we are given the gift to recognize the possible adverse or positive significance of any situation.

Using Multiple Lives to Your Advantage

The expression, "Everyone has a second chance" is not quite right, in reality you have an infinite number of chances. God in his all-embracing love provides you with as many retries as you need for you to attain your goal.

I have read in Spiritist literature, that when we are in the womb, forming as a fetus, all of us automatically relive all of our past lives, from the first to our highest level. I believe it serves to reinforce our determination to demonstrate a better performance than our last.

What is reincarnation but a trajectory of an increasingly perfected routine, much like an ice skater practicing over and over again. Every minuscule mistake must be removed and each session should be better than the last.

Perhaps that realization that we are on earth for a mission, a duty to be accomplished is why I have my earliest memory. I have never told anyone about it. Therefore, it wasn't implanted in me like the false memories of many events for children.

I was in the crib. I know this because I saw wooden bars when I opened my eyes. I must have been in a heavy sleep. I saw a feint light in the room and I thought to myself, here I am.

That was all, a confirmation of myself that I was here. Why have such an obscure memory if it wasn't to set the task before me. Like a soldier departing the landing craft and stepping onto the beach, there was a moment of awareness that to live I had to keep moving forward.

Since then I have been marching on, most times in not so good order, more like an overweight and ill-trained civilian, but advancing nevertheless. Secure in the knowledge that not to move is to stagnate and to die on the beach without accomplishing the objective.

The Supreme Intelligence is patient and just, nothing will happen to you that isn't there to make you a better person. Isn't this the hardest concept to swallow? Intellectually most of us can understand it, but emotionally, when pain and disappointment occur we are thrown off our balance, like being on a ship in choppy waters.

I started off handling my down periods by thanking Jesus for the opportunity to learn. At first I would say this sarcastically, like in the vein of, "Thanks for nothing!" But just speaking the word "thanks" helped.

Next, I graduated, to not only mouthing the word but thinking. Feeling and visualizing gratitude. Slowly my sophomoric stance disappeared and I found myself accepting and reflecting on the trials I experienced.

I began to listen, actually hear what I should be hearing from my conscience. Trying my upmost to block my baser self from rationalizing why I should ignore what is right.

Using my conscience as my wise old mentor, a mentor with thousands of years of accumulated knowledge. A library that has a case study to interpret even the thorniest of situations, which can be conjured up at any time. Far superior to whatever you could find on the internet. It is always present, even when your despised internet carrier is down.

Leverage what is inside you. You have a wealth of life experiences. Be deaf to the words of others who love to tell you what they would do, careless of the consequences. Listen to yourself. Meditate and pray for guidance. It will be given to you. Because most of all, the spirit realm loves you and wishes for you to raise yourself in this life to prepare you for a better life in the next.

Chapter 4 - During our Lives We Pay for Past Debts and Accumulate New Experiences

Have you ever had kidney stones? A female nurse told me that she believes they are the equivalent to child birth, without the ending joy. To this day, I wonder what I had done in a previous life to deserve it. It must have been quite bad and I promise I will never do it again, whatever it was.

I remember like it was yesterday. I was at work when I started to feel a sharp pain in my side. I tried to suffer through it, but it increasingly worsened. I left work and walked to the ferry. I live on an island and take the ferry every day to my job.

I managed to make the half mile walk. I sat on one of the ferry benches. There were plenty of empty spaces, since this was around mid-day. Then a very strong attack occurred and I couldn't find any way to sit to lessen the pain.

Nice people came up to me and asked if I needed help. Finally a nurse came over and asked me some questions, and then he said it is probably kidney stones, and that I should go to the doctors right away. Pain medicine would be of great assistance.

I called my wife to see if she would meet me at the dock, so she could drive me to the doctors. After I finished my call, a ferry worker told me to wait until a wheel chair could be found so they could take me off the ferry. I thought what a nice thing to do.

I waited in my seat, writhing in pain, when everyone else walked off the ferry. Finally, for what seemed like hours, but it was just a couple of minutes, a ferry worker came with a wheelchair.

I envisioned being rolled across the gangplank and down the hundred yards to the area where my wife was waiting to pick me up. As soon as we got off the gangplank, the ferry worker told me, this is as far as I can take you.

I waited extra time in pain to be rolled about thirty feet! I got out of the chair and managed to make it to the car. In five minutes I was at the doctor's office.

In the small consultation room waiting for the doctor, I was on my knees with my arms resting on a chair. My wife looked at me and told me that she remembers this scene. When she had her Near Death Experience (NDE), she saw herself at the doctor's office with her husband on his knees in great pain.

I fulfilled my destiny by prostrating myself in pain. And as a bonus I had the added lesson of the anticipation of being assisted, but not really.

Payback is not Supposed to be Fun

My illness was pre-planned; I was to feel the emotional equivalent of what I had, in an earlier life, inflicted upon others. To those who don't believe in karma, I would advise you to rethink your stance.

In one of the books that the spirit Andre Luiz dictated to Francisco (Chico) Xavier, Andre visits the Reincarnation Ministry and discusses a plan for a man about to be reincarnated. The official at the Ministry points out a dark spot on the subject's intestines and tells Andre that when the man reaches his forties, he shall have a painful ulcer. In his previous life, he had stabbed a person in the stomach and he shall relive the pain he had caused another.

During a Spiritist presentation a woman's case was being discussed. In her later life, she had severe pain in her lower body, so bad that doctors had rigged up a cage like apparatus to hold her lower torso and legs in place. It was almost as painful without the harness.

Why the suffering? The woman, who in her present life was a wonderful mother and a patron for the poor, she participated in multiple charities. She raised her children to all be fine upstanding adults.

Even though, she was relatively virtuous in her current life, she still had debts to pay. She was a queen of Spain, during the time of the Spanish Inquisition. Although, she didn't directly order the torture of people, she allowed it to take place by signing arrest warrants brought to her by Jesuit officials who were fully aware that their victims would be egregiously tortured.

This is a perfect example of a reason not to wish to be a queen or king or any type of nobility in your previous life. The more powerful you are, the more capacity you have to harm others.

It all comes back to us. Look there is no other way to say it, payback is not pleasant.

When you are in the middle of such a trial, remind yourself, what the other person must have felt and promise to never hurt others again. Try not to whine or complain. If you can refrain from doing both, then you can have the smug satisfaction of being absolutely superior to me!

At the end of the trial, like the man standing in the doorway as the building collapses and he escapes unscathed, you can take a deep breath and feel elated that you made it out alive. One more payment completed, never to be visited again.

For every debt paid off, it is one more ugly episode which will not follow you in your next life. Take comfort that as you learn your syllabus those classes are forever behind you.

When you see others going through trials, please don't say it could be worse. It is what it is, no better or worse than what was destined. Listen and empathize. You can because you have been through painful trials too and had no clue why this was happening to you.

Silently, say a prayer to help the person persevere through their assignment. Stay positive and your attitude will be transmitted to all around you.

Schadenfreude and Why You Shouldn't Have a Little Pleasure

I love the German word schadenfreude; pleasure from the misfortune of others. Doesn't the mere existence of that word capture the state of the human race in a nutshell? We are like the kids on the playground who snicker and are excited when we see someone else get in trouble.

We need to sympathize with others during their misfortunes because whatever they have done to deserve their current state, we have probably committed the same or worse error.

Now that I have said that, there is a little immature spark in the back of my mind. Which I promise to erase someday, but for now supplies me with justification to accept with resignation the indignities that are heaped upon me.

When I go to work and hear about the latest idea to fit us into ever smaller cubicles, so that at some future date, we employees would be jealous of the poor caged chickens who are fatten without ever being able to turn around, I think of the people making those decisions.

I shake my head and reflect on what awaits them. Is there some futuristic sweat shop in their next life, where in the morning they are enclosed in a foul smelling body suit and not let out until all required hours are logged? I certainly hope so. No not actually, well for a moment or two.

I check my conscience and determine that instead I should take pity, for the decision makers don't understand the ramifications of their actions. He or she is thinking of immediate rewards of being singled out as a star cost cutter. Maybe they will receive a larger bonus or an extra percent of increase at the end of the year.

Their boss is hoping that by squeezing more out of each employee the stock will rise a couple of pennies, thereby enabling the purchase the yacht that he or she craved. Because you can never have too much.

After all, they are being pushed by Wall Street for ever increasing profits and however you do it is fine. Just keep shoveling more money their way.

What these fine souls do not realize is that gain on the backs of others is temporary and the reward will not justify the bill that will be due at some future date.

Many deserve their wealth. They have contributed to society's good by ethically employing workers and treating them with respect. The amassing of capital to undertake large projects is also to be lauded. The wrong comes when the quest to maximize profits crosses the line from honorable to dishonorable, fair to unfair, equitable to inequitable treatment of fellow humans.

We are Also Here to Learn

There will be periods of your life where you will meet a situation that you are not prepared for and the going may be difficult. Take heart, this is a training exercise.

The Doctrine of Spiritism tells us that our goal is to become a pure spirit. A pure spirit has no need for a physical body. A pure spirit is mostly composed of energy and very little matter, who is able to move at the speed of thought.

Jesus is a pure spirit. During his time in a physical body, he healed the sick, walked on water and fed thousands from a few baskets of food. It is said in the spiritual plane that when he spoke he implanted visions into people's minds. This is why individuals flocked to his sermons.

A pure spirit is a powerful being. Imagine if Jesus had not been good. Imagine the harm he could have inflicted upon the poor and weak.

I look at myself and think what I would do if I had that power. I try and concentrate on performing wonderful deeds of charity and assisting those in dire need. But in the back of my mind, I ponder, what could I make if I just went to Las Vegas for a weekend, the slot machines would pour forth and the dice would do my bidding.

The free drinks wouldn't even require any of my special powers.

Am I ready to be a pure spirit? Heck no! Sad to say, my years of compulsive schooling are still ahead of me.

So it isn't just to pay for past wrongs that we are here, it is to be thrust into many different scenarios. We are in a flight simulator. The purpose of the simulator isn't to practice a smooth landing over and over again. The reason a pilot spends time in a simulator is to experience every possible calamity.

A good pilot will have been trained to recognize the pattern of danger intuitively, before others even notice events are turning ominous. As soon as the red lights start flashing, the well-trained pilot will have taken counter-measures to repair the situation.

Wouldn't you love to be like that? You will. This is why you are here on earth, in a dense body, having every possible emotion flay you alive at every second. Pretty darn good training, isn't it?

As we ascend in our spiritual quotient, our courses become increasingly complex. Same as an undergraduate student discovers the next level of expectations when he or she enters graduate school.

Take heart and realize the seven tenets of Spiritism are on your side. We aren't just delivered to an orphanage abandoned and alone as in a Dickens novel. We are surrounded by love and constantly guided by our spirit mentors.

Our trials are selected with our benefit in mind and never forget this point; every test is created so we will have the means to be victorious. Again, there is a way to win in every situation. It may not be what our culture believes is winning, it will be what the spirit realm knows is winning.

To come out on top doesn't mean that we have pushed others underneath the pile, but that we have raised others, we have brought ourselves up a level in goodness, love, charity, and fraternity.

We are supported, not only by spirits, but by our spirit friends and family who have decided to come on this great adventure with us. We are part of a club of immortal friends who stand by through thick and thin. We may not recognize them at every turn, but they are there.

Some Training Works Best on Earth

I often sit back and pose the question, why can't we just learn in a classroom setting in the spirit world? Why do we have to suffer here?

Unfortunately, there is a very good answer. The spirit world, at least the higher realms, is vibrant, colorful and full of loving sentiments. A perfect location to acquire knowledge and partake in intellectual exploration unfettered by the type of limitations we are bound with on earth.

But that is precisely the drawback. The emotive turmoil is not present. It is like trying to bake bread without heat. The ingredients are there, but heat causes the chemical reactions to occur to bring forth a full, pleasant smelling and tasteful loaf.

The spirit realm has a saying, "Pain is the great teacher". I wish it wasn't true, since I don't desire pain to be a part of anyone's life. Pain doesn't necessarily mean the smashing of your finger in a window, but the emotional pain of living through hard lessons, seeing injustice done to yourself, your family and to others.

Suffering focuses the mind to commit to change. We know this is true. In fact, we use this very technique on our children. When they perform some dangerous or wanton act, we at first try reason. Very quickly we then determine when a calm approach is not working. Then we raise the stakes and punish, either by withdrawal of toys, standing in a corner, or a good talking to. In our minds, we aren't inflicting real pain, but in the child's mind something very bad has happened. They know there must be a change. Hopefully the child will learn to do better, without any lasting ill-effects.

God has given us the gift to use our emotional stress as a

facility to modify our behavior and more importantly our thoughts. A gift that is not readily available in the real, the spirit world, where we live for the vast majority of our immortality. That ability to train our minds via the fire of emotions is why we are here on earth.

Paraphrasing the words from a high spirit in one of Andre Luiz's books (psychographed by Francisco C. Xavier), we are like clay models, who require the heat of the kiln to set in place, forever, the divine attributes which we all seek.

The More You Help the More You Will be Helped

Whenever we, as individuals, or collectively desire to attain a goal, we frequently attempt to engage others to help us to fulfill our objectives. The people we attempt to bring onto the team are ones that we have worked with before. Seldom do we seek to enlist the aid of strangers, since their willingness and capacity are unknown to us.

Relationships are key in this world and the same goes for the spirit realm. To foster spreading a supportive network, we should in turn demonstrate our ability to provide for others. Via direct help, prayer, a shoulder to cry on, advice at the right time or a multitude of possible encounters. We should be willing to invest our time when a cry for help is heard.

There is a story, again in an Andre Luiz book, about a man, who had dedicated his life to helping out. He became very ill with a painful skin disease. A team of spirits was attending this pious benefactor.

One of the team members asked why is this man going through his suffering. The explanation was that in an earlier life he had caused his workers great discomfort by the conditions he made them work in, and now he had to live through the same.

Then another spirit appeared at the man's bedside. He pleaded with the group to ease his suffering, because the poor afflicted man had just recently helped his widowed mother buy medicine for one of her still living children.

He had done so, without question and without prompting, handing over some of the little amount he had left from his pay. The leader of the team explained to his staff that this is why they were here, by the selfless deeds he had performed, the trial he had requested himself, so he could pay back his wrongs, would be lessened.

All good comes back upon us. The Supreme Lord has set up a virtuous cycle which reinforces blessed acts with more.

Often it is hard to spot its existence in our world, but it exists and it is a force of heavenly benevolence. One has to only consider your own life to come up with examples of good repaid with good.

During one of my jobs in my career, I was managing a very complex and stressful project. I had everyone working extremely hard and focused on the task at hand.

One of the men who worked on my team had a child. He was so busy that he didn't register their newborn baby within the thirty days required to place the baby on their insurance for the rest of the year.

Can you imagine how anxious you would be if you couldn't have your newborn on your own insurance? My poor co-worker would have been a wreck for the entire year.

He went to Human Resources and asked if they could at least contact the insurer and request an exemption. Human Resources came back and said no, that is the policy and we won't request it.

I went and pleaded with them to give the guy a break. It was my fault; I kept the team working many hours. They wouldn't budge.

I went to the President of the company and asked him directly. He called HR and told them to request an extension. HR called and the insurance company said it was no problem.

You would have thought that would have been the end of the story. One of the HR managers called me in to his office and proceeded to tell me, without ever looking into my eyes, that I should never do that again.

I told him, that I would do it again and again. Why couldn't HR apologize for their mistake, after all, a short phone call solved everything. From that day on, I was a marked man in that organization.

I knew I had to leave. It was amazing how fast I found a new and better job. Never in my life was there such ease in interviewing and negotiating for a higher salary.

Looking back at it, I am sure I was placed in the hands of spirits who eased my transition from one job to another. By sacrificing my potential career at one company I earned the right to start anew at another.

Chapter 5 - We Live and Learn in Close Family Groups

When I met my wife, after only two weeks of being together, we were at an ice cream store on Copacabana beach, when she told me that we would have a destiny together.

It was a Häagen-Dazs store. Very expensive for Brazilians at the time. Which could explain why it disappeared several years later.

The sun was setting and the surf had a calming rhythm which added to magic of the moment. I saw but didn't hear the traffic, only the wind and the gentle motion of the waves.

The air was warm but not stifling, a perfect tropical breeze kept you refreshed. The sea smell was that pleasant mixture of the lure of swimming in a warm salty ocean which would wash away the cares of the world and the connection with the vast oceans of the planet. As if one could travel anywhere by just swimming a few strokes.

Silently, I told myself, yes we do have a destiny and I shall marry you. Little did I know that we had been married before.

Exactly How Many Wives, Husbands, and Children Have I Had?

With multiple lives, not to mention multiple spouses within each life, the list could be a cast of thousands. Imagine one woman could be responsible for the entire Nation Football League given an average amount of children through thousands of years.

A bit frightening, it is not? I can barely remember my children's names, I keep calling them by the dog's name at times, which shows my power at keeping things straight.

It's funny, when I was a kid I couldn't figure out, why couldn't my dad even call me by the right name? Now I know.

I am going off-track here and yes I know you want to find out how families are grouped together, but first, let's talk about pets.

Animals have spirits too. They also have multiple lives. When Chico Xavier was sitting next to a woman, he noticed she had a dog on her lap. He asked the woman, "Do you know how old your dog is?"

The woman replied, a bit incredulous, "Of course I do, he is about three years old."

Chico smiled and told her, "You have had your dog through multiple lives for over five hundred years."

Whereas, one could say in each life the woman had a dog, in fact she has had only one. A pet that has travelled with her through good times and bad.

This is why, when you had that one special pet, and they pass on, the feeling is never quite the same with the next one. There was a special connection, strengthen by shared existences.

It is the same for family too. This is not to say beloved couples stay together for eternity. No, there is a natural progression, when one spouse elevates and journeys to higher planes, the one staying behind will find new ties of love. Or the spouse who has ascended will actively assist the other to make the climb.

The important point, is that as we ascend higher and higher, our love becomes special for all beings. It is true indiscriminate love. Every soul has a special place in our heart when we have truly reached the state of a pure spirit.

But for us on and around the earth, we have a more limited range of that special love and affinity. We still cherish our immediate family.

In the books, psychographed by Chico Xavier, dictated to him by his spirit mentor Emmanuel, there are reoccurring characters. Actual accounts of spirits who have reincarnated into different physical bodies over the centuries.

In fact, a group of people who were originally introduced in the book, *Two Thousand Years Ago*, and later in the book, *Fifty Years Later*, were reused to provide Chico a job in the twentieth century.

Chico's spirit guide, Emmanuel, was a Roman Senator during the time of Jesus. He met Jesus and Jesus asked him to follow the new doctrine, but Emmanuel declined, due to his pride of being a Roman, the most powerful people on earth.

In *Fifty Years Later*, Emmanuel is reborn as a Greek slave, serving, you know the answer, a Roman. It is this Roman family that can be used as an example of how intimate groups are reincarnated together, but with the deck of cards reshuffled to teach each member the life lesson they so sorely require.

The basic characters of the story is a Roman husband, proud and powerful, his name was Helvidius Lucius, his wife, Alba Lucina. Their daughter Celia was a secret Christian.

A woman named Claudia Sabina who although married, loved and desired Helvidius, and her maid Hateria. Claudia later maneuvered Hateria to become a maid in Helvetius's household, so she could better plot the destruction of their marriage.

Claudia and Hateria, were eventually successful in severely wrecking the marriage of Helvidius and Alba, by sowing mistrust and causing the exile of one of their children.

Let's fast forward about one thousand nine hundred years. Helvidius Lucius, now reborn in Brazil, as Romulo Joviano. He was in charge of a government farm, where new methods for ranching and farming were developed and tested. His wife is Maria Joviano, who was Alba Lucina, in one of her previous lives.

We have a husband and wife who have loved each other and been together since the time of Christ. When people talk of a soul mate, this is exactly what they are trying to express.

A love that doesn't just span decades during our lifetimes, but a love that transcends mere physical bodies, time and space. A love that is replayed upon the earth, to create a family where others can see their examples and children grow to maturity in a loving environment.

In their Roman existence, they had a daughter, named, Helvidia, who once again returned as their daughter, with the new name of Wanda.

So your children, your little precious cargo, those that give you so much love and so much worry, could well be your offspring from multiple existences. They, your closest friends in the spirit world, volunteered to return to life as a dense form, so they could be raised in a loving family and be prepared to face their trials with a firm foundation of love and learning.

Not only are your children related to you in ways you haven't perceived, but also your parents. The parents of Alba during her Roman era were her same parents when she reincarnated in Brazil and grew up with the new name of Maria, who, by the machinations of the spirit world, would once again meet and marry Romulo.

Chico Xavier worked on that farm. That was his day job, for most of his life, until he retired. Chico's spirit guide, Emmanuel was part of Romulo's household, as a slave one thousand nine hundred years ago and was now directly involved with the same family. Except Emmanuel was in the spirit world and the family was in their dense physical form, travelling through one more lifetime on earth.

During the Joviano family gospel gatherings, of which Chico was invited, they would frequently receive psychographic writings from Emmanuel. Spirits who work together in the spirit realm, will continue to work together. Even though some may still reside in the spirit world and others in the physical world.

Here is the twist to the story. The Supreme Intelligence, in their Divine Wisdom, is constantly trying to show us the error of our ways and provide situations where we may improve.

The woman, Claudia Sabina, and her maid, were reborn as

sisters to Romulo (Helvidius at the time right after Christ). So they could learn to love Romulo in a sisterly manner and to repair the damage they had caused in another life.

Both women grew to become good and charitable people. Although, throughout Romulo's life, the original Claudia, never liked any of Romulo's girlfriends and particularly didn't approve of his eventual wife, Maria. Some habits are particularly hard to break.

A family web is woven that lasts not one mere lifetime, but of centuries. Intimate groups of souls that have worked side by side, supported each other and shared experiences that spans epochs.

This is what you are born with. When you feel all alone and abandoned and no one understands you, think that in fact, you are surrounded by loved ones, who know you only too well!

You think you understand each person in your household and every facet of their character. You actually know them better than that. In reality, deep down in your conscious, you instinctively feel when they require help, are fine on their own, or available to assist you.

Your Instincts

How do you recognize your central family characters so well? Besides taking your conscience with you in your new life, you also bring your instincts. From more than thousands of years of experience, where you have succeeded and failed in a multitude of situations, you have built up your sixth sense.

I use mine every day. I try and listen to that little alarm bell. Once when I was in Brazil, I walked in the morning to the bank to withdraw some cash. As I approached the building I felt a twinge, a warning to be careful. I looked around and saw nothing.

I kept heading toward the bank. It was before the bank opened, but it had the front area open for those who wished to use the ATM machines. It was about eight o'clock in the morning.

I usually withdraw money in the morning when I am in a foreign country, on the premise that the robbers are habitually active during the dark hours and that by morning, they must be tired after a hard night of taking advantage of innocents. Even thieves have regular schedules.

I opened the door to the lobby and stepped inside when I definitely felt a caution. Just inside, I stopped and looked around one more time.

The second scan of the perimeter was the charm. I spotted the would be thief concealing himself behind a newspaper kiosk. He attempted to appear as if he was reading the morning news.

In fact he had the appearance of having an unsuccessful evening and was trying to make at least one score before giving up for his work day.

I turned back, patted my pockets as if I had forgotten something and exited the bank. Out of the corner of my eye I could see his expression. He must have thought that once again he had bad luck today, since his mark must have forgotten his bank card.

My instinct had saved me. By listening carefully to your feelings you can avoid many dangerous situations. Divine Goodness has packed many tools for us to use in our journey.

In the tenets we have learned so far, our immortality, the love that bathes us, the lives we have lived all serve to increase our awareness of every possibility. Without realizing it, with each life we are becoming veterans of survival.

The Supreme Lord that is managing us does so with the utmost caution in mind. We are not sent on to our life in a dense body alone and without methods to triumph. Sense the panoply of instruments which reside inside of you, learn to rely on them and life will open like a flower to the sun.

Jumping in with Both Feet

The opposite of avoiding dangerous situations is true too. Do you find that sometimes you will uncharacteristically throw yourself into a position that ordinarily you would have avoided?

Of course I am excluding those exceedingly dumb periods we all have, where we don't listen to our instincts, our conscience, or anyone else around us trying to save us from ourselves.

I am talking about an urge to go further than you have before, either with another person, an objective you are pursuing, or another endeavor.

I was like that when I was with my wife at the ice cream store. My instincts said to let go of my normal caution. It had to, why else would I let myself get involved with a woman in a foreign country that I had only just met. It was madness!

I went to Brazil on business and met her while on a tour for a few hours after my meetings were completed. I felt an instant attraction. Of course, being a man, I regularly feel an instant attraction. But this was different, it was more than a surface desire. Some unknown force drew me to her.

It was as if the needle of my instinct gauge went from "Maximum Caution" to the opposite end, "Absolute Abandon all Caution". My rational brain signaled me to slow down. My thoughts and my instinct usually collaborate to function as the governor for my baser emotions. This time everything was out of synch.

I was already planning my next trip to Brazil as I was ending my business down there. After a little more than a month I was back. This time on vacation and free to spend my time as I wished.

The experience at the ice cream store sealed the deal for me. I was hooked and started to think through when I could come back again. My instinct had released me from all restraints.

It did so for a very good reason. I was with my soul mate. The person who I have had relationships with in previous lives and in the spirit world.

Through these magical processes families are reunited. Husband and wives are reunited on earth, so they may bring their children with them to begin once more the course of life lessons which are in front of them.

Somehow, I found my soul mate. I grew up in Southern California, right next to Disneyland, never traveling out of the country until my teens, while my wife was raised in a large family about one thousand miles below the equator.

It is as if two darts were thrown at a spinning globe. Wherever one landed one of us would be born. Then the fun in the spirit world would be to figure out how in the heck we can get these two to meet.

One never knows in what environment you will encounter your real family. They could live anywhere, be of any race or culture. The outside covering isn't important, what is vital is their soul. Their past history with you is the fulcrum upon which your destiny is levered.

I know of a family that adopted a child. They had one child but wanted another. When all attempts were exhausted, they decided to adopt a boy. The family are Spiritist. They were curious to determine the spiritual heritage of their new son.

The family went to a Spiritist Center. There they were given the message that their new son is actually their old son. It was determined to send him to the family by an alternative method, since the spirit world knew his mother could only have one child.

Now, when I talk to parents with a diverse family, step-daughters, adopted sons, all combinations, I tell them you could all be related in ways you may not realize. Your step-daughter may have been your real daughter in a previous life. Your instincts will tell you the truth.

Start with loving all and let your feelings spread out to every family member, you shall soon determine those who have had a previous relationship with you. It will be that extra little spark in your heart. A bit of certainty of the extent of your love even when times are tough.

Exceptions to the Family Rule

I mentioned earlier where a rival and a willing accomplice to destroy a happy marriage where born into the same family group which they tried to break apart. Now they wouldn't be a competitor or a lever for destruction, but as children of the couple.

Why would our Supreme Father want to do this? Because, we are being trained to love everyone. And yes, that means even those we really detest.

And those we just scorn, make fun of, try to avoid, gossip about, point out as a bad example to our children, and even give an occasional dollar to on the street, all should be loved.

I know, it's hard enough to love those who you actually love. Your objects of affection can be very trying at times. The urge to throw them out of your sphere can be extremely powerful. Don't, having your patience tried is one of the tests.

All couples and families have rough spots. Fights can get very intense. Just remember, we are here on earth to help each other. Sometimes, letting others make bad decisions, even after vigorous counseling is a trial they must travel through. Be there as a support, even after the consequences befell them exactly as you had predicted.

In one of my past jobs, there was a person, who just drove me crazy. She questioned every action I took. Her inquiries weren't polite, they were posed like the accusations of an inquisition. I knew she spoke out of malice not out of wishing to help.

I complained to my boss. He told me that a part of my job was to make her happy and that I would have to deal with it. The best advice I could have received, although at the time I hated it. I was now mad at her and my boss.

Quitting my job out of spite wasn't an option at that juncture, so I talked to others. I found out she had a consistent grating approach. No one liked how she grilled them. But the bottom line is that she exposed many faults early on in the process and was a valuable member of the company.

I buckled up and decided to record every suggestion. I did this for a few weeks and then I created a report on her suggestions and the responses. How we would mitigate each possible risk.

I took the report to her and she was delighted. No one had taken the time to exhaustively document each detail and the response. From then on we worked closely together.

She never did learn how to question with kindness, but I overlooked that and grew to respect her talent and admire her intellectual ability.

Ridding yourself of that powerful, yet destructive emotion, hate is freeing. Your body feels better and all of your vital centers can function in harmony. Attempting to understand and work with others in polite discourse is imperative.

The penalty for failure could last several lifetimes. The spirit world doesn't allow for unresolved major disputes. If they exist when your present life ends, the thread will be picked up again in in the spirit world or in your next incarnation.

Jesus didn't tell us to forgive seven times seventy for an idle reason. He knew that to become a pure spirit you must learn to forgive and ask for forgiveness. All previous battles between two souls must be concluded.

If you and your adversary can't resolve your dispute, the spirit world will do it for you.

When I was growing up, my sister and I would fight. My mother's solution would be to lock us both in the bathroom and not allow us to exit until the fight was over and we promised to not fight again.

I hated that! Who in the world would want to be locked in a

room with a person you detested. But, the threat of living out my entire life in the small bathroom overcame my stubbornness. I would grudgingly offer my apologies and she would do the same. Then I would be free, until the next altercation.

I didn't realize at the time, that my mother acted exactly like the spirit world. They hand out Divine Justice by a similar method. Except, you aren't lock in a room, you are intertwined by family bonds.

Where you will either grow to love each other, as you should have done before, or you will fail the test and have to retake it as many times as you need until you get it right.

To avoid having your bitterest enemy as your brother or sister, or even your father or mother, or child, in your next life, clear your palate of all desires for revenge, justice, hate and envy for enemies in your life.

Our Divine Leader metes out all justice. All souls will receive the classes they require to be able to comprehend the extent of their own wrongs. You only need to sit back, improve yourself and support others.

Families Volunteer to Help Less Developed Spirits

There is another type of person in your family who doesn't quite fit in. This person usually displays an immaturity in many areas. They find it harder to delay immediate gratification. They are more prone to violence. They are clearly not in control of their emotions.

When we are in the spirit world, we recognize our duty to assist our less advanced brethren. Couples who plan to reincarnate, meet up, and marry will often volunteer themselves to raise a spirit who requires direction to the correct path.

Children are pliant beings and have been constructed thusly to allow parents to mold their character. Immature spirits who have the opportunity to enter a family of more advanced souls have a valuable gift.

Many families spend considerable effort in managing the education of primitive souls. Many are successful and receive the blessing of knowing they have contributed to one more needy soul. Others less so, but the very fact they attempted to help is acknowledged by the spirit realm.

All of us can cite an example of that one child who clearly did not fit into a family. When I was growing up, we had a family near to us. The mother and father were great parents and people. Their kids were bright and pleasant, except for one. The oldest.

He just could never get anything right. His parents worked hard to get him through high school. They tried to get him into college, but it just wasn't going to happen.

He became a drug user, then quit drugs and turned to alcohol. All of his problems were caused by the world. Never himself. He would come over to his parents' house and the neighbors could hear him yelling at his poor mother and father, blaming them for all of his failures.

His parents tried their best. They did all that they could have possibly done. Their son exercised his free will and decided to not let his family environment influence him to the good. He will have more opportunities in subsequent lives.

On a Mission

Some children are born into families that have no ties with them, not because they need help, or had a past altercation, but are there on a mission.

These children are the opposite of the ones who were less advanced. Child who come to families, so they can be born into the right place at the right time, seem to almost raise themselves.

They are often calm and dutiful children. They are more intelligent than their siblings or their parents. In fact, these young souls will frequently serve to assist their parents in their material and spiritual life.

These little lights of life are a bit harder to spot than the black sheep of the family. But they exist and they have come to earth to help others. At the same time, they still may have debts to pay and lessons to learn.

Children born into a mission will be more actively guided by the spirit world during their lifetime. When a soul volunteers for a specific task on earth, the help they receive will be commensurate with the job at hand.

As one of the seven tenets of Spiritism, you now realize your family is even more complicated than you thought before. There aren't just currents surfacing from past arguments and situations, but from past lives, past entanglements and encounters.

Your family is also a more intact and loving group than you have realized before. Not only are you tied together by blood, but by a more important connection. Your family is bonded together by shared experiences that span thousands of years, in a variety of cultures, countries and social circumstances.

Your family has been fused into one by the accumulation of shared trials. Trials that have tested each one of you to your maximum endurance. Nothing can replace the camaraderie of soldiers who have survived life in the foxholes.

You have that gift, you may not feel it at times, but it is there deep within your heart. You know your family is precious. Now you are able to open your heart and your eyes to the extent of your love. A love that doesn't disappear when one of the clan dies, they only move on to the spirit world, where they await you, to begin anew your cycle of incarnations and ascent to become a pure spirit.

Chapter 6 - Our Destiny is Mostly Predetermined

Growing up I always wanted to be an Air Force pilot. I had plans to enter the Air Force Academy and graduate flying fighter jets. My goal was to become an ace, I didn't care against whom and any enemy country would fit the bill.

My father was in the Army Air Corp during World War II. Did I get my desire to be a pilot from him? Not exactly, he was a sergeant, albeit a highly trained one. He worked on the hydraulic systems for the first United States jet fighters.

In fact, he and his buddies were on a ship loaded with top secret jet fighters bound for Europe, when the war ended. My father didn't waste his top secret status. Only he and a few of his buddies were allowed to look beneath the tarps covering the jet engines.

Taking the opportunity in hand, he hid cigarettes and silk stockings inside the engines. Later he was able to trade these rare commodities for diamonds. Black market diamonds that his sister used when she got married, much to my mother's everlasting disgust.

He did see action though; when he was dealing with a trader in a partially burned out building, a competitor took a shot at them. My father ran down the stairs, saw a German policeman, took his rifle, and ran after the culprit. He never got a good look at who tried to kill him.

On my mother's side, her brother was in the army before World War II. He didn't like it much so he decided to travel to Tijuana, Mexico to recover his inner peace. His sergeant found him and brought him back.

From that proud tradition of military service, I too wanted to play my part. All was going according to plan until the end of my junior year in high school.

I noticed that I wasn't performing at sports like I used too. When playing baseball I would miss the ball more often. In the outfield I would lose the ball in the air. Finally, my father recognized the problem and took me to the optometrist. I discovered that my 20/20 vision had left me.

The optometrist also told me that I was righted eyed and left handed. I asked, "What does that mean?" and I was told that meant I was a mixed up kid. He was correct, I was at a crossroads; my career plans were destroyed by my poor eyesight.

I thought about becoming an officer in one of the other services. A friend of the family arranged to have a Marine officer come by the house to talk to me. He knocked on the door and my mother saw him and straight away told him I wasn't interested. I never got the chance to talk to him.

I don't remember her ever doing anything like that to me before or afterwards. On her own she eliminated one of my options.

Instead, I decided to major in Computer Science at the nearest University of California campus, at Irvine. My life trajectory took an entirely different path than the one I had envisioned.

Being Guided on Your Path – Your Body

One could hear a story like mine from most people. Small things cause minuscule course corrections, whereupon they add up to where we embark on an outwardly random road. But, stories similar to mine perfectly demonstrate the levers used to guide us in our predetermined path.

First, through the pre-planning process; before I was born, my body was designed for my mission. Not just the base genetic code that I inherited from my parents, but subtle modifications were made to predispose me for my mission.

I was predestined to experience changes that would occur within certain time intervals, time bombs that go off when I reached certain ages. Impossible you say. Not according to the

Spiritist writings I have read. For years, scientist believed that there was lots of junk in our DNA strands. Many items in our DNA didn't have any relevance to our initial creation. Now there is emerging evidence that there must be some purpose for these seemingly useless bits.

Well there is a purpose, many of our major health issues are pre-planned to occur. My eyesight for example, or worse, my kidney stones occurring at a certain age. All there to invoke a reaction which serves to begin a new trial or move us to a different phase in our life.

Physically we are pre-programed. With our soul deposited into our temporary bodies, we are fitted into spacesuits which enable us to live on this hostile environment that are preset for our tasks that we have been assigned to by our Divine Benefactor.

Not every event, accidents can happen, and we can exercise our freewill to harm the bodies bequeathed to us, by smoking, over drinking, or a myriad of alternate ways to degrade our performance.

The marvelous aspect of all of this is that each and every one of us has been sculptured by expert hands. We have been created for a purpose. We have come into this world equipped for our required lessons.

The aim is for all of us to succeed. No trial is created so that we are certain to fail. We are always supplied with the resources to attain the objective. The other tenets remind us of that fact. We are loved. And help is constantly at our side, just waiting for a call.

Being Guided on Your Path – Influences

This takes us to the second gentle method to herd us in the right direction. When my mother, closed off any avenue of going into the military, the door was opened to start at the University in a major which would allow me the means to work toward my goal.

Almost immediately after giving up hope because of my eyesight, our high school received two calculators, which could be programmed by small cards. This was before the advent of the personal computer.

I became enthralled using these programmable calculators. My math teacher was amazed when my friend and I were able to program the quadratic equation, where the user just had to enter the variables. Eureka, I found my next passion.

One door closed and another opened. How many times have you heard that expression! It's true and for a reason you have not heretofore known. The spirit realm arranges gifts and whispers into people's ears to shape events.

I am sure my mother had the undeniable impulse to swiftly dispatch the innocent Marine officer, planted in her mind at the moment she answered the door. To her, it was her idea, but not actually, it was a suggestion from a spirit, guided by the Supreme Intelligence.

The new equipment the school received; all planned. Not only for me of course, sure it had other uses, but one of its purposes was to take part in my little life comedy.

The realization that Divine Providence is involved in micro-managing our lives alters everything. No longer can you consider yourself a ship afloat on the ocean, rudderless, being moved by currents and tides.

You are here for a purpose. A very important purpose, otherwise the amount of expense and supervision would not be at the level it is. Your life is a precious commodity and considerable effort has been expended on your behalf.

If I said that your life was predestined, but never mentioned the other tenets, then having a pre-defined blueprint for your physical life would make no sense. One can only arrive at predestination in context that we are loved individuals on a training mission, or more aptly, sent to college with a curriculum all filled out by our guardians. Watched and managed to keep us on the right track.

There is a wonderful Spiritist speaker Haroldo Dutra Dias,

from Brazil. He tells how he was subtly maneuvered into his present profession. He was talking to his mother-in-law about careers when she suggested he take the Brazilian exam to be a judge. He expressed no interest and thought the idea would be boring. He had other plans.

Finally he picked up the literature which explained the contents and the required knowledge for the exam. He thought he should take the test to please his family and have an option to fall back on.

Everything clicked. What he read before the exam seemed to prepare him for the test. During the test, he knew everything. His recall and analytical powers had never been so good.

Now he is a judge. He has time to research and give speeches on Spiritism. He laughs about his trajectory. We all should, we are like animals running in a maze who reach the food in the middle, totally unaware of the doors being opened and other pathways closing, allowing only one choice.

To us, life is a series of random events, unrelated to anything else in the universe which in a chaotic manner put us where we are now.

We had a sheltie when my daughter was about three years old. He had a very strong herding instinct. We had the usual home with a front lawn, a sidewalk next to the street, a driveway and a small wall flanking the lawn. When my daughter would play with her friends, the sheltie would keep all of the children on the grass, never letting them onto the sidewalk or the concrete driveway. As they ran around in their playfulness, they had no clue they were being herded within a confined area. We are no different.

Freewill

Unlike the children being controlled, we can step off the grass, if we ignore all of the warning signs. We can change the arc of our lives. The penalty for doing so is that we must, in some future life make up the lessons we skipped.

The hard part is to recognize the signs. If your conscience

keeps telling you you're doing the wrong thing, listen to it. If night after night you have anxious dreams about the path you are currently on, then it's time to reevaluate. If the alarm is ringing from your instincts, heed it. If those closest to you repeatedly warn you and you are certain they have your best interests in mind, you may want to actually listen to them.

Before I met my wife, I began a relationship with a very nice woman. Everything seemed to stop me from being more involved. I was never so sick in my life, one cold, flu or whatever after another. We had planned a mini vacation together, on that day her car acted up. We cancelled the trip. She took the car to the service station; they couldn't find anything wrong with it. The car never had that problem again.

I was being guided to not begin a serious relationship with that particular person. I was being held in ready to meet my future wife.

I could have ignored all of the signs and exercised my free will to stay with a different woman than what I was intended to be with. Thereby, losing my chance to fully pursue my destiny. Or, thankfully, I recognized the signs, warnings which piled up and all pointed in one direction, that it wasn't my time to be with that person.

It was difficult and painful, but in retrospect it was necessary for completion of my trials and probably hers too. By allowing myself to flow with the current, the events propelled by the seven tenets of Spiritism, knowing that I exist in an environment of love and that my intended plan is what I need to grow in my present life, I am able to gracefully accept the vicissitudes that come my way.

When I am depressed about some lost opportunity, which will never come my way again, or a failed chance to start a meaningful relationship I try and climb up on that high mountain and look down at my life. Not just my present life but my immortal spirit life too.

I ponder on where I am now, how loving, charitable and

fraternal am I? I try and realistically place myself on the low end of the scale of all three. I shudder thinking how much worse I must have been before. Then I give thanks to be at least at the level I am now, where I have begun to listen to my conscience and do what is right, not what is expedient.

Next I analyze where I would have been now if I hadn't been guided and led to the lessons I so sorely required. Would I still be an uncivilized taker of whatever I want? Immune to the feelings and wants of others, spreading destruction and unhappiness wherever I traveled? Most certainly, yes.

The trials I had subsequently must have been dramatic and violent to bring me to my current state. I am sure at those times I cursed the universe for my troubles. But now, where I foolishly consider my obstacles to be major, I am gifted with a superior life and an improved ability to follow my conscience.

I return and peer down on the path I had trodden in this life and for better or worse, I am where I am. I have acquired knowledge and empathy. I have a greater appreciation of the problems others go through. Have I attained my dreams and been allowed to follow my passions? No, those were valuable lessons too.

As a pruned tree grows stronger, when we deny ourselves and deal with the termination of a dream, we too are sturdier, more resilient to withstand the waves that crash upon us. Each step forward in our current life, that we take based on solid moral principles, we plant another foundation stone. We advance on our quest to become what we are destined to become, a pure spirit.

Then I try and peer beyond my current state and imagine my life in the spirit world and my next incarnation. Every step up brings more responsibility. As Jesus says; to those who are given much, much will be demanded. As we grow, we are expected to contribute in proportion to our capabilities.

I tell myself that the pain and suffering I endure now shall result in a marvelous situation, where I will be able to support others more fully, guide the downtrodden more effectively and be tasked to perform good works, where I will gladly show up every day, ready, with my friends to be of service.

Eventually, my path of lives will lead to a place where hate, envy, and destructive selfishness are all left behind. Where what we are and the good that we perform is more important than the trappings of wealth that are displayed.

This insight stills my emotions and places in context my worries. One day I hope to automatically maneuver my apprehensions to the correct bucket, but for now, in my less advanced state I will do what I can. I will strive and continuously move forward with the certainty that the Supreme Lord and all of the spirits in its service is guiding and following my movements for the best possible outcome.

Interventions

Many times the spirit realm will actively attempt to get us back on the right track if we seem to be veering off in the wrong direction. Nothing illustrates this better than people who have had Near Death Experiences (NDE).

One of the recurring themes of people who went through a NDE is that they learn they do have a life plan. They recognize they are on earth for a purpose.

This epiphany often irreversibly alters the life of the experiencer. They don't allow the constant ups and downs of normal existence to distract them from their intended purpose. To learn to become more loving and caring, while assisting others. They come away from their NDE intuitively knowing the reality of the seven tenets of Spiritism.

One such example is the NDE of a man who had a heart attack. He left his body and was led through a beautiful forest by a lady. He came to a clearing in the woods. There was a large oval table, with eleven people sitting, seemingly waiting for his arrival.

He didn't recognize anyone, but he had the feeling that he knew them and they were all friends. He was welcomed and told that his life would be reviewed to determine if he had completed his assigned tasks on earth.

The group or council as he described it, had access to every moment of his life, not just the two-dimensional scenes, as if in a movie, but a full transcription of all that occurred, down to his thoughts and feelings.

The council examined episodes from his life to discover if he had acquired the knowledge and new found attitudes which were important for him in his present life. They also showed his actions from the view of others around him, not only the participants point of view, but their thoughts and feelings also.

The council wanted to judge the emotional effect of his actions upon others. Imagine a world where everyone strives to insure that others are always supported and made to feel loved. That even when a person needs to be redirected, they are done so with the most delicate hand possible. This is why we are here on earth, so we too may mold our behavior to become a constant positive force.

The talent of pushing people to better perform with a velvet glove instead of an iron fist is difficult. I find my first instinct is to demand immediate change from a person. I should think first and look back if this approach was ever successful when it was directed at me.

No, it wasn't, I got mad instead of marshaling my forces to change myself. All I did was to try and change the outside world to fit myself better, while I should have spent my effort to modify my outlook and attitude.

After examining pertinent scenes from his life, the council and he both agreed that he had not quite developed the skills that his plan of life had laid out for him. He had to continue to follow his life blueprint. His education was not over yet.

He was directed to return, but to do so with an increased spiritual awareness. A heightened ability to break free of the material chains and to place more emphasis on his and others spiritual health and wellbeing.

Our friend who had a heart attack was given a magnificent gift. Divine Justice intervened and notified him that his education wasn't complete and his classes would continue. They discussed his triumphs and failures and set him back on earth with renewed faith. They provided him with clear directions for success. Nothing could be more beautiful or profound than this act by those that love us.

There is another case which demonstrates how we are notified of our areas of improvement to concentrate upon and then put back on track. A woman who had a near death experience met her spirit guide. He led her to acknowledge her failings.

In her NDE account she tells us that she has had problems with her temper and her ability to forgive. She was shown, through the eyes of the people she rudely encountered, what it felt like to be on the receiving end of her admonishments.

She entered their innermost emotions and for the first time discovered the effects of her words upon her targets of abuse. She felt the desire to be loved and admired by the very people she belittled.

Yet, she writes through her whole ordeal of watching her tirades and unfair criticisms pointed at innocents, she never felt personally chastised or attacked. The entire review didn't feel like an emotionally draining meeting with her mean self, but an uplifting instruction of the need for love and caring for all.

She felt the love of the spirit world, the immense blanket of supporting arms for each one of us and she desperately wished to be a part of it. A light went on in the deepest part of her heart. She began to look at every action she took from the other side. She realized the vital healing properties of positive thoughts.

She learned that to modify another person's behavior doesn't have to be accomplished with a stick, but with a carrot. I am still trying to follow this example. All too often I slide back and lash out, breaking my own moral code. Afterwards, I meditate and ask for guidance and patience. I plea for the opportunity to just slow down and think about my actions before I commit a wrong.

When she returned to the land of the living, things changed. She cleaned out all of the old possessions that didn't agree with her new life. Any book, magazine, or music that didn't supply the positive vibrations she sought were discarded. She spent more time concentrating on her family and less time shopping.

She no longer craved the minuscule therapy that acquiring materials goods provided. For the first time she understood the relative importance of her spiritual side and her material needs. The more she did without unneeded objects the better she felt.

Her health improved and her family life thrived. Divine Love intervened and gave her the tools and desires she required to pass the classes, surmount the hurdles and survive the trials ahead, so she would be able to emerge from her temporary assignment in her body into the real world, the spirit world, victorious.

For those few, blessed with an unforgettable sojourn in another plane, the seven tenets of Spiritism are as real as night and day. Their life is forever altered. Never again will the small annoyances hold power over them. Yes, there will be always some setbacks, but on the whole, their approach to life is the view of one from a high mountain. Looking down at the entire arc of the journey, not the rocks that litter the path, but of the flowers that lie ahead.

The love which supports, pushes and guides us to our destiny. Our immortal life, in which we train for the glory ahead by short visits to earth.

Missions

While we all have a plan for our life, for some of us, our trials to correct past wrongs is interspersed with a higher goal. The goal is set by the spirit world. It always entails a task which will serve to better humankind. The ultimate goal is to promote our culture to rise to the desired level to bring the earth up from a planet of atonement to a planet of regeneration.

Collective humanity is presently still in a mode of learning how to be civilized. Therefore, the earth is used as a campus, like a laboratory within one of our universities, to train all of us. As part of our training, we must pay for our past wrongs and learn how to behave in a true enlightened society.

One day, when enough of us are fit, the earth shall become a place where we will still incarnate to study, but our training shall be relatively painless and more emphasis placed on the accumulation of experience to round out our preparation for our next evolutionary step toward perfection.

We volunteer for these missions. We may never realize we are on an assignment. During our childhood and the stages of an early adult there may be no clues whatsoever. We would be guided by the spirit realm, while remaining completely unaware of our true purpose.

Only through retrospection and analyzing the events that took place and where a person ended up can one discern a pattern that points to a purpose beyond mere personal improvement while on earth.

Sometimes the message is crystal clear. When Francisco (Chico) C. Xavier was approached by his spirit mentor, Emmanuel, he was told he had a choice. He could devote himself to Spiritism and the works of Allan Kardec or not, it all depended on his free will. But if he chose Spiritism, he would have to do three things, work, work, and more work.

Chico selected work; so much work in fact that he ended up psychographing more than 450 books, all the while holding down a full-time job to support his family. He only retired when he was in his sixties, after working since he left the 4th grade.

I know of a woman who possesses mediumistic abilities. Her use of her talents were for the benefit of others, but were unfocused; there was no grand aim in mind. One day she heard of a shop with a Crystal Light bed, sometimes referred to as Crystal Light Therapy. She signed up to use the bed, thinking it would serve to relax and soothe her entire body and psyche.

She asked the lady in the shop how she should use it. The woman told her to use it an hour a day every day for a week. She began the therapy and after a few days started to feel a team of spirits perform major psychic surgery on her body. Afterwards she had never felt so exhausted. It was as if each day she had a major operation and wasn't allowed to recover before she started the next procedure.

When she was finished, she asked the clerk, does everyone use the bed every day for a week? The woman answer, no, she just wanted someone to try it that way so she could see what happens. Well, something grand did occur and it set her and her husband off on a voyage of discovery.

Through one of those synchronistic events described by Jung, which we now know is the spirit world manipulating events, the couple got in touch with me. They had discovered Spiritism and wished to learn more.

Now, they understand they are on a mission and have responsibilities ahead of them. They are fully cognizant of the assistance granted to them by the spirit world and welcome the opportunity to serve.

When Jesus came to us, he told us that he came to serve, not to be served. That is precisely our goal. Not in this life, we are too engrossed with just making it day to day. We haven't reached the state where we can start our journey with a set of clothes and a good pair of shoes and trust in God to deliver our needs.

I am not there yet. I am too preoccupied with looking ahead and making sure I have the mortgage covered and enough left over for food and supplies. I haven't yet mastered the art of floating free on the current created by the seven tenets of Spiritism and letting it take me where I need to go.

I am learning and slowly freeing parts of my inner compulsive self. One little hesitation at a time. I recognize I won't be able to master it this lifetime, like a naked Indian Guru who sets out secure in the knowledge that he will be provided all that he needs.

That time will arrive, of that I am certain. It may take multiple lifetimes, but I shall attain my goal. How do I know? Because thought is action, as a spirit, my thoughts transfer into material deeds, when those contemplations are based upon faith and love, I will be helped to my destination and watched over during my entire journey.

Chapter 7 - We are Assisted in our Lives by Unseen Spirit Forces

My dog, playing roughly in the bushes, somehow managed to tear her dog tag off her collar. I, being the lazy person that I am, procrastinated getting a new tag with our telephone number on it.

My wife and I went out to the grocery store, just a quick run for a few items. When we returned our dog, Neve, was missing.

Neve, which means snow in Portuguese, is a white Canadian Shepard. A wonderful animal, friendly and smart. She is also a professional shedder. If we stopped vacuuming the house, within a month we would have a thick carpet of white dog hairs.

I have always been reluctant to have a dog. Of course my wife and mostly my two children wanted a dog. They made all of the promises that children make, they would feed it, clean up outside and personally groom whatever cute little animal we purchased.

I was having none of it, I let them know the exact length of their previous promises. The goldfish that died, the hamster that they were bored with after a month. All broken promises. They cried out in unison, “But this time it would be different!”

Knowing my intransigent stance, the family stealthily waited until I was out of town. They went to a pet shop and found a cute little puppy. A tiny ball of fur that the pet store owner promised would never shed, or maybe just a little bit.

Upon my return I was trapped. Puppies are hard to resist and my defenses crumbled immediately. Of course a month after we got the dog, my wife and I were the ones who did most of the maintenance. But by then, Neve was one of the family.

Usually when Neve gets out, she returns after twenty minutes or so. She likes to visit the other neighbor dogs and mark her territory. When the children returned from school, she still hadn’t found her way back.

We walked around several blocks, crying out her name. No answer. We all trooped in the car and drove around a wider area. Again, no sight of her.

Back home, everyone was in dire straits. We feared the worse that she was lying in a ditch, the victim of a car running over her. We all prayed for her return.

Ten minutes later my son's friend phoned him. He told my son that his mother had looked at the local veterinarian's web site and saw a notice about a lost dog. She immediately knew it was Neve.

We called the veterinarian's office, but it was closed by that time. We got in the car and drove to their building. We walked around calling out Neve and finally we heard her familiar barking.

The next morning my wife went to the vets and collected a very relieved animal. I talked to my son's friend's mother. She told me she never goes to that web site, but so some reason she felt the urge to look at the veterinarian's web page. She instantly found Neve's picture and told her son to call us.

A lucky coincidence? Could be. I would never have thought to look at that particular web site. I had no clue that our local vet posted lost dogs on their page. The wonderful woman who called, had no apparent reason to bring up the web site either.

I choose to believe that our spirit mentors, our beloved guides sprang into action and by whispering in the right ears, they arranged our reunion with the family pet.

For many this would seem a trivial event. Why the vast spirit world would be interested in helping a family find a lost dog is beyond their comprehension. After all, if there is a God, his or her interest in us must be extremely remote or non-existent.

This small episode of kindness perfectly illustrates the true extent of the spirit world into our lives. For our lives to be predetermined, for events to happen to us at the right time in the right order, an army of spirit workers is required.

Each of us are managed and guided by a platoon of bright shining spirits all motivated by their desire to be of service. Spirits on the ground, spirits supporting them, spirits maintaining all the infrastructure required to direct our trials on earth. An immense undertaking, all to take immature souls and mold them into civilized productive souls.

Once you internalize the true state of the world and why we are here the seven tenets not only begin to make sense but they must be present. Unless we are immortal, how could it be possible for each soul to improve in just one lifetime? Unless we are loved, why would we be guided to learn the lessons we require? Unless we are allowed to return time and time again how can we absorb the classes assigned to us? Unless we must experience the suffering that we have caused others how could we really learn? Unless we stay in close supporting groups how else could we survive the hard times and gain the loving foundation to keep moving forward? And finally, unless our curriculum is carefully planned how would we be able to concentrate on fixing our deficits?

All tenets depend on the others. All work in concert to grow rough seeds into beautiful flowers. As any gardener knows, you don't plant seeds and walk away expecting to find a flawless row of blossoms awaiting you. A garden takes work and attention. Weeds must be pulled and water provided.

We are objects of constant attention. Great events and small happenstances are arranged for our benefit. All meant to push us just a tiny amount forward.

Money Comes When it is Needed

Others too find events occur at the right moment. A postmaster found his niece was communicating to him at her funeral. At first he wasn't sure what was stirring in his mind. A voice called out to him for help.

The voice appeared to be like a four-year-old's, which was how he was thinking of his niece while at the funeral. She actually died in her twenties. He stood up and left the room, trying to orient himself. In the corridor, he thought, "Why are you talking to me?"

His niece told him that she tried to talk to everyone, but he was the only one who heard. Then he asked, why she sounded like a four-year-old. She replied she could sound like any age and proceeded to speak like a teenager, herself and as a senior.

He was overwhelmed by this plea for help from beyond. He was forced to rethink his entire outlook on life and for the first time recognize the certainty of life after death.

After the funeral he helped her talk to her mother. He allowed his niece to speak through him to her mother. He had discovered a hidden talent.

He began to help others who had spiritual problems. He particularly helped veterans who had PSTD (post-traumatic stress disorder). He continued to assist people after he retired.

When he talks about his experiences he says he helps without expecting recompense. He learned to not worry about money because somehow the money always arrives.

He is able to live and dedicate himself to others because the spirit world works behind the scenes to gather opportunities for him to make a decent living. That is one of the small miracles that is gifted to us by the spirit world.

By giving, he receives. He created a positive feedback of virtuous thoughts and deeds. The more he dedicates himself to the good, the more good will come back to him. Unbeknownst to us, our worthy behavior is rewarded.

I was interviewed by a woman who had an internet blog. We were talking about reincarnation and how the spirit world is actively involved in our lives.

I told her about the Postmaster and how he said that the money comes when it is needed. It was a moment of clarity for her. She then proceeded to tell me her story. She too had a near death experience.

She was so altered by the episode, she couldn't return to work, instead she dedicated herself to helping others. The disability payments she received from the government wasn't adequate for her needs. She recently was given a house to live in as part of a job watching a park.

As we were talking, she realized she had been rewarded for her efforts by the spirit world. The free stay at a home wasn't a lucky happenstance, but a planned compensation. A token of her personal impact on the lives of the people she touched.

Take comfort that at the end of the day when you are exhausted from helping others, without receiving a word of thanks, for your perception is false. While it would always be nice to be personally thanked, that gesture is actually just a salve to our selfish desire to be acknowledged. More importantly, your deeds are recorded and applauded by the spirit world.

You have scored one more point, advanced one more step in your quest to become a more loving and caring person. That is a victory no one can ever take away. And it is a triumph worth more than the temporary luxuries that money can buy, for with each advance your rise in the spirit world is cemented.

The Spirit World and Your Dreams

Have you ever thought of a problem and couldn't figure it out, or had strong emotions that you weren't able to let go? Then, after a good night's sleep, the solution to your problem was at hand, or you were able to work out your emotions to your satisfaction?

The answer to how that works according to most would be to say that your brain was working on your problems as you slept. Well yes, that may be partially true, but what is actually happening is that your spirit is the one responsible.

Think of your body as a spacesuit. It is needed for you to function here on earth in this dense material dimension. But nobody would like to have to be inside that cramped, slow-moving spacesuit twenty-four hours a day.

When we sleep our spirits are free to leave our body and roam around. Our spirit go to where we are thinking. Those erotic dreams you had, they were probably acted out with other spirits who were like-minded.

You travel to where your thoughts take you and to whom your thoughts take you. The speed of light isn't the universal speed limit in the spirit world, the speed of thought is. You have considerable freedom, within the bounds of earth to journey to various locations.

Most of your dreams that you remember are jumbled fragments and have no meaning for your daily life. When you left your body you had no objective in mind.

There are times when our minds are focused. Our feelings, like a laser, are aim at one object. We may silently be asking for guidance. We turn over a problem again and again, seeking an answer.

The spirit world hears these muffled pleas. When we sleep, spirits come to us and take us to places to discuss our problems. They will bring other spirits with them to craft a solution.

There is an example of this in a book psychographed by Francisco (Chico) C. Xavier, *Missionaries of the Light*, a young woman, with small children lost her husband and was inconsolable. To supply her closure with her dead husband, the spirit world arranged a visit with him, during her sleep, when she could leave the bounds of her body. She was able to talk to him and find out that he was safe in the spirit world.

Since, our spirits can communicate directly with other spirits during our slumber, we learn many valuable lessons and have various conversations with other spirits, spirits who could reside in the spirit world or other incarnates, who had left their body.

We are unable to retain exact memories of these encounters. But we do awaken with general ideas and feelings. Just like the widow did from her sleep, when her aunt asked her if she actually believed she visited her husband in a dream the night before:

> "Why not?" replied the widow without blinking, "I still have the feeling of his hands on mine, and I know that God granted me such grace so that I could find my strength again to work. Today I woke up totally refreshed and happy! I can face the future with new hope! I will make an effort and I shall be victorious."
>
> "Oh Mommy, how your words console us!" exclaimed one of the little ones with bright eyes. "How I wish I could have been with you to listen to Daddy in that wonderful dream!"[11]

When you arise in the morning from a satisfying sleep and you feel good for no apparent reason, this could be a residue from a nocturnal encounter you had. Or when you leap out of bed ready to tackle that problem which had been bothering you for days, this could be the result of you finding out the solution while talking with your friends or guides in the spirit world.

If we search for the answer it will come. The spirit world wishes to supply us with all of the tools and inspirations required to prosper while we live on earth. They fully realize the day-to-day problems we encounter, complications which hinder our ability to absorb the lessons we should learn.

Like any good teacher, who wishes their students to be successful, the spirit world gently pushes us to the correct solution. We have to listen carefully to what is going on around us. We should analyze our dreams to find clues to what path to take.

Before I started writing this book, I had written four books concerning Spiritism. Each one discussed different aspects and referenced many passages from the available Spiritist literature translated in English. All meant to bring forth essential concepts to enable one to fully comprehend the Doctrine of Spiritism.

One day, a woman in our Spiritist group suggested I write a more accessible book on Spiritism. I should speak with my own voice and be personal about the effect of Spiritism in my life and the life of others.

I wasn't comfortable with the idea. I enjoyed staying in my ivory tower, researching and writing about concepts, not personal actions and emotions.

Then I had a dream. My father was in it. The pattern that I have noticed is that any dream with my father present is significant. Also, during dreams with my father, he never speaks, we are just together.

I am not sure if this is because I am incapable of retaining any dialog that I hear during my wandering as a spirit outside of my body or if it is planned. All that I have been able to ascertain is that I have never had a meaningless dream when my beloved father was part of it.

I dreamt that I was a passenger with my dad at the wheel. We were in a SUV. He began driving on a regular paved road. He drove normally, in the middle lane of a three line highway.

One other constant in dreams with my father, is that he is always the driver and I am the passenger. Which, as I write these words, make total sense. For I am the one being taken on a journey. I am being led by the far wiser spirit. I sit on the passenger seat, not in control of anything. My job is to sit, watch, listen and learn.

I sit on the right side looking out of the window, enjoying the warm desert air. We are in an area which is similar to the highway on the way to Palm Springs from Los Angeles. Where the desert begins in earnest, close to Beaumont and Banning, which lies in Banning Pass.

Not the developed cities they are now, but as they once were in the seventies and eighties. Sleepy towns with a few fast food restaurants to serve the tourists who need a break on their way east.

Suddenly he veers off the road and crashes through a flimsy gate. The SUV handles perfectly well in the desert gravel. I tell my father, "Dad, what are you doing? Get back on the road."

He returns to the asphalt and we are proceeding as decent responsible drivers should. I get back to my routine as a passenger, which is to feel the air and look at the silhouette of the highlands in the distance. Dreaming of walking through the clear mountain meadows.

Again, with a sharp right tug at the steering wheel the car is off-road. Gravel is flying and we approach railroad tracks. With a bump and a slight crashing noise, the SUV leaps over the tracks and onto a side road. The dirt track ends and we are driving through native desert habitat.

The dream ends. I wake up and think, maybe I will write that other type of book! I had been comfortable on the highway I was on, I needed to get off on a different path.

Welcoming Assistance

When we receive aid, we should take a moment and reflect on the enormous task that planning, guiding, supporting and tracking just one poor soul must be. Are children at all thankful for the effort invested in building schools, training teachers, arranging field trips, writing books all for their benefit? No, they see it all as a burden, just like us. We see life as suffering which we must withstand, with flashes of joy interspersed to keep us motivated.

This isn't the case at all. Unlike children, we must open our eyes and see, for the first time, an entire world created for our express benefit. A world that has our education as its primary purpose.

A legion of dedicated teachers, putting up with our sophomoric behavior, investing daily in our education. We only have to open our eyes and see the small incidences, the dreams we have to spur us on, the ideas that pop into our heads to know we have a support group around us beyond our wildest imagination.

Ask and you shall receive; a key message from Jesus. Little did we discern how true it is. Ask for guidance and it will be given. You merely have to stay awake and recognize when what you have requested is delivered.

Once you spot it, follow the trail, Let the seven tenets be your driver. Sit in the passenger seat and listen to the lesson at hand. Enjoy the view while you are moving along the path that so many have travelled before and will travel after us.

Chapter 8 – Moving On from Here

I had a dream in 2011, before I became immersed in Spiritism, it was the first time in a long while that I had one of those vividly real dreams, where I didn't know I was dreaming. I was in a car. I was seated in the passenger seat. This was the first dream I had with my father since he died.

My father was driving, on Walnut Street headed toward Ball Road in Anaheim, California, also known as the home of Disneyland. It was a familiar road that I travelled many times on my way to school, work and friends. I can't tell you how many times I either rode my bike or drove my car on that street.

On the road you saw the back end of the Disneyland Hotel; in fact, many years ago there was a 9-hole golf course, which I played as a kid, with my cheap bag and about four clubs and a putter. I remember watching the dragon flies around the small ponds, as I fished out my errant golf ball.

As you passed Cerritos Avenue, there was an orange grove, flanked by Eucalyptus trees on one side and a farm on the other. My father, growing up in Monrovia, California, then an underpopulated suburb of Los Angeles, would drive down the middle of the road. No doubt from his early years of driving on deserted streets.

My father was driving in the middle of the road. As usual, I felt a bit exasperated with his technique, but having learned long ago that commenting didn't rectify the problem, I just hoped we didn't front-end an on-coming car.

We didn't speak. Walnut Street ended at Ball Road, there use to be a small office at the end of the intersection. It was a house that was converted into an office. To make it look official there was a fountain in front. More times than not, I would drive by and see that some kid had put detergent in the fountain, so the round fountain would be filled like a bubble bath.

In my dream, the fountain was full of bubbles. Then somehow

we walked into a small sports arena. I have no idea where the arena was or how we got there, we were transported to the front door and started walking in.

Inside, a basketball game was playing. As my father and I walked past the wooden stands, the arena was the size of a high school gym, the score board show Home – 5 and Visitors – 14. At the moment that I stepped into plain view of everyone in the arena, the crowd stood up and cheered, even though the basketball court was empty at that moment.

I never spoke with my father, I was only with him. This was enough for me. There was no better father on the planet.

What did this mean? Two years later I began reading The Spiritist Book, by Allan Kardec. In 2014 I started my Spiritist blog. I have published four books and now this is my fifth book. Who knows? The meaning could be entirely different from my current impression.

I do believe that this book is a marker in my life. I will proceed in a different direction, which road will be presented to me, I know not.

I am certain of one thing. The seven tenets of Spiritism are like the gravity of the Sun, planets, and the Moon has on earth. There are invisible forces that keep me on a path. There are unseen currents that float us down a river that we do not detect, but are there nonetheless.

Your life and well-being is influenced by the spirit world following the plans you laid down. Let the love of the Supreme Lord and the adoration of his servants guide you. Events will happen that you may believe are serendipitous but are in fact subtle pushes and pulls to your current direction. Sequences of occurrences that are called by a name: Synchronicity.

Synchronicity is not just a concept coined by Carl Jung, which he created to express the seemingly random events that are meaningfully related, it exists and he intuitively knew it must have been caused by a higher power.

Synchronicity is real and the spirit world is the invisible force behind it. The seven tenets all work together to enable our life to have meaning. We are in the middle of it, we may miss the overall theme, but it is there.

Living with the 7 Tenets

What do you do when you are caught in a current or an undertow? Do you swim against it and perish by exhaustion? Or do you swim with the flow and keep swimming until you reach a safe harbor? There is only one answer for survival.

We are told by lifeguards to swim with the direction of the current and never, never ever, give up. All else is futile. All else is a waste of time and energy. And yet, many people die exactly in that manner, attempting to beat a natural force hundreds more time as powerful as a swimmer's puny strokes.

We see friends and acquaintances every day that seem to fight what life brings them with all of their power. Not the challenges, such as being born into poverty and working your way out honorably. No, I mean persisting in performing a wrong or non-productive act, all the while being thwarted at each corner, but never giving up. I admire their dedication, but it is misplaced. Unbeknownst to them, the spirit world is trying to help them, attempting to deflect their path onto a productive endeavor.

I think back at the time I had lost my job at a bank that was closed by the FDIC, during the Great Recession. My wife had told me before to relax; the bank would be hiring me back. How did she know this?

At the age of fourteen, her godmother told her that her husband's bank would go broke and he would be hired back by the same bank but with a different name.

But could I rest with that information, even though her predictions always came true? Of course not, I allowed myself to be stressed and anxious. I had good reasons, the job market was horrible. I sent resumes everywhere. When I started to get job interviews I was happy, for before whenever I had an interview, the odds of actually receiving an offer were heavy in my favor.

I wasn't so lucky, every interview I attended, they called me back for more. At each company where I went through an extended process, I always came in second. This went on until, you guessed it, I was hired back by the same bank, but with a different name.

I was swimming upstream, against the current, losing valuable time pursuing that which I would not be allowed to gain. Instead of using the time to increase my skills or my spiritual side or just be with my family, I threw the time away.

How do you recognize when you should desist? I haven't a clue. It is a fine line between being a quitter and accepting that your chosen path is not right. I do know that if you have chosen an objective that is against your conscience and you have rationalized why this is necessary and your plans seem to be blocked, take this as a warning and stop.

The opposite is true. When you are on the right path, gifts will be presented to you, opportunities will arise and you shall feel you are doing the right thing.

When my wife and I started reading about Spiritism, we found a meeting in Seattle. We enjoyed the group, but the drive and the cost of the ferry trip was a hard burden every week. We were thinking of opening our own little group on Bainbridge Island.

That summer we went to Rio de Janeiro. My wife, Ana, and children went ahead, since I could only stay for my vacation time. Ana went to a book shop and she was looking at some Spiritist literature. The owner came up to her and told her about a Spiritist Center close to where we were staying. She wrote down the name and then forgot about it.

When I arrived, after a week, I suddenly had the idea that we should visit a Spiritist Center in Brazil and see how it's really done. Ana dug out the name from her purse and we decided to go.

We showed up and asked the first person could they help us by explaining what they did there. He looked confused and said he would find someone. A wonderful woman took us under her wing. Not only did we tour the facility, we went to some of the nightly meetings and she invited us classes on mediumship.

Everything fell into place. We all went to a Spiritual Healing Center in another state. All the usual roadblocks and miscommunications were absent. It was meant to be.

We helped by being open and resisted the urge to say no and went with the feeling and said yes to everything. We let the flow take us and we weren't disappointed.

Winning with the 7 Tenets

The plan for your life, constructed by you in cooperation with your friends in the spirit realm, is meant for your benefit. If you would just keep your arms to your side and refrain from touching the guardrails the ride would be smoother. Being human, we have a propensity to expand simple problems into complex ones. We love to tinker and change on the fly.

Recognize the signals ahead of you and follow their direction. Don't fight the flow of your life, follow it and see what marvels will be revealed.

Simplify

Instead, we should strive to simplify, divest ourselves of unnecessary encumbrances. When you embark on a trip do you take everything you could possibly want or do you pack what is essential? The same is true for our life. We are on a short training exercise. We don't need much and we certainly aren't allowed to take anything back with us.

When I started out in life, I was caught up in the culture to consume and to accumulate material goods. My happiness was tied to the number of toys I had. I ran up credit card debt and the associated stress. The emotional lift from my new acquisitions never outlasted the repayment schedule.

Slowly, I modified my habits. I asked myself two questions: 1) Do I really need it? And 2) Is this going to make me spiritually better? It's amazing how often the answer is no. By casting off the anchors that tied me to the earth I allowed myself the room to let others in. I cherished the time with my family and friends more and didn't lose sleep over what I was missing that someone else had.

As a modern bobsledder wears the type of suit that drastically cuts down on drag, so he or she can speed down the hill just a little bit faster, releasing extraneous goods smoothens our ascent and removes the hindrances that slow us in completing our trials. We and our spirit guides can concentrate to getting us to where we should be.

By removing distractions, I noticed the little signs that were sent to me. Instead of anxious dreams, I felt refreshed and calm after a good night's sleep. I listened to what people said to me and I began to identify those who were put on earth with me so we could work together.

Spotting the friends and family who are your boosters, the ones who don't care what you have but who you are, is a giant step. I started to categorize the people who consistently gave me the same advice as my conscience. The ones who wish to draw out the good.

In High School I had two such friends. We reinforced each other to do what was right. When I cheated on a spelling test, my friend called me on it right away and I never did that again. Looking back on it, we must have known each other in the spirit world and in a previous life. We three were in tune with each other.

I went through a period where I hung out with a different crowd. I remember one incident, where one of my "friends" was driving recklessly, I thought to myself, why I am here doing this? This isn't fun and we could inadvertently hurt someone. Most of the time was spent in trying to get others to perform something stupid.

Thankfully I woke up and realized that the fun they seemed to be having was only fun to them. To me it was a waste of time. But I did lean on them afterwards for valuable instruction. Whenever I wasn't sure of the right thing to do, I posed the question to them and always followed the opposite of their advice. It never failed.

These cherished allies will drift in and out of your life, for everyone has their own plan and we will cross paths only when it is called for. Learn to spot them and value them. The individuals who tell you the truth and suggest ways to stay on the right path are there, like hidden treasures in a video game, to assist you to be victorious over all obstacles.

Ask for Guidance

When I am stuck and can't find a way to move forward I ask for guidance from the spirit world. Sometimes I ask Jesus personally. I know that when I make a request with humbleness and sincerity, I am tapping into the immense spiritual reservoir of love. Love that is always present and ready to help.

Little things materialize when you ask for help. For instance, we all have lived through those annoying times when we are looking for a certain key phrase or section of a book, but we just can't seem to find it. We know it's there and it must be hiding from us. When I am working on an article about an aspect of Spiritism, invariably when I think of a reference I wish to cite, I open up the book and find it quite rapidly. Believe me that hardly ever happened for me before.

Big things too. People will appear that lend you just the right advice or opportunity at the exact time you needed it. I remember the time when I was a senior in High School, I wasn't sure what major I wanted. I thought about it going back and forth from math to history. Not really thinking that either one was the right choice.

Then I went to a gathering with my parents. At the party there was a professor from a nearby college. He came up to me and started talking about choices for majors. He explained about this relatively new major, called Computer Science. Immediately, I thought about how I loved working with that primitive calculator. Bingo! That was it for me.

Did I actively pray for guidance at that time in my life? No I didn't, but the spirit world picks up your thoughts and desires and your unvoiced pleas for help. I am certain now they arranged the meeting and inserted the right people at the right place so I could choose the right path for my life.

This is what is wonderful about living in the seven tenets. Learn to use the power of the hidden resources. No one wishes you to succeed more that your spirit guides.

They are sitting on an unseen bleacher out there, cheering you on. Ever ready to lend a hand.

Positive Thinking

A spirit is their thoughts. What they look like, the clothes they wear, the aura they emanate all begin with thoughts. A being composed of mostly energy possesses great power in their minds. Higher spirits are capable of complex manipulation of matter.

Thus, in our goal to one day become pure spirits, we must strive to control our thoughts. It isn't enough to keep our mouths shut and not let harmful words spill out, we must start at the source.

This is actually easier that it would seem at first. When I walked to work I would see derelicts sleeping on the sidewalks in the little nooks and crannies that any large city has. I would look at them and think, what a bum! The world would be better off without them.

Now that I realize they are souls, just like me, in the midst of a trial. For them, a trial on earth that has gone horribly wrong. I spot them and I say a little blessing. I try to add one small positive thought to assist the poor souls during their hardship.

If I have learned anything in Spiritism, it's that whatever I have seen a person do something that I disapprove of, I have probably done worse in some previous life. So who am I to judge? I am just a little bit farther on in my multiple life plan.

The other exercise is to not jump to conclusions about the performance of people. For example, my wife had to make travel plans to fly internationally. She found out she needed a new passport. We had hints from the spirit world that this is a voyage she would make.

We quickly got the paperwork together and sent off the completed application by the fastest and most expensive method possible. My wife added a note asking for expedited service, explaining that she had to travel because of a death in her family.

We expected the passport to arrive the week before the flight. We felt secure because we believed we would have assistance by our spirit mentors.

But the week went by and we became nervous. She was due to fly on Saturday and by Wednesday we were talking about how terrible those people are at the passport office. How uncaring and typical of government workers. And why would we have to rebook the flights, if the spirit world wanted her to travel?

On Thursday the passport came, with the note my wife put in. On the note the date when she would have to fly was circled. Everything happened according to plan. Only we didn't have faith and we lapsed into blaming innocent people, who were at that very moment working to allow us to make my wife's flight date.

We should have remained calm and accepted that if the passport didn't come on time there would have been a good reason. We wasted time and energy, when we should have remained positive.

Being confident and optimistic is the key to succeed during any trial. Sometimes that is all you have. Your ability to remain hopeful and to not lose your love for others during periods of great stress for you is a measure of your growth.

Remember we are surrounded by support and that the hurdles

thrown in our way of are of our own construction, designed to make us better souls.

Put Everything in Perspective

Every so often, climb up to the fifty thousand foot level and look down at your life. Pretend you are a wizened old soul who has seen and done it all.

Look at the beginning and trace your path to the present. Contemplate the hurdles that you had overcame and the moments when you unnecessarily believed you were absolutely defeated. Then think about the better opportunity that came your way.

There isn't just a silver lining to every dark cloud, there is a golden reward within it. When times get bad, you should get excited, anticipating the marvelous present that will soon be delivered to you.

During the aftermath of the year 2000 anticipation of global catastrophe (which would be caused by two missing digits, 19 or 20, the first two numbers of a year), that never occurred. Technology companies started to feel the effects of the ending of the first internet boom.

The smart money, which started it, was pulling out fast, leaving the rest of the world holding the bag, as usual. I was working at one such new internet company.

I could tell the bottom was dropping out, but I figured that it still had a few years to go before the end. Then the terrorist attack of September 11th occurred and overnight all business halted. That was the sign for those on their last legs to give up and liquidate.

I was out of a job and on the street. Everyone else in technology was too. A less than perfect time to find new employment.

The dark clouds were swirling around me. Since, I knew that no employment could be found for the rest of the year, I decided to travel to Brazil. A country I always wanted to visit.

I grew up loving the music of Brazil 66, and somehow just never made it to the other side of the equator.

Almost broke with no prospects for employment I went ahead with my plans. Just as I was getting ready to pay for flights and arrange a hotel, I was called by a consulting firm and asked to fly to Rio on a business trip. It was for a company that I had worked for in the past and knew well.

I visited their headquarters and we agreed upon the objectives of the trip. I couldn't believe my luck. How could everything be brought into place so efficiently and quickly?

Within a week I met my future wife in Rio. When I returned the company wanted me to consult for an extended period of time. My life started on the trajectory to where I am today. All brought about by the machinations of the spirit realm.

Whereas, I could have stayed put and concentrated on my pitiful state, instead I went with the flow and kept moving. The spirit world had plans for me and unless one continues to strive in life nothing can be attained.

I exercised my freewill in maintaining a positive attitude and was able to grasp the objective in my next trial. Whereas I could have ignored the signs and remained closed to the world and missed the best present of my life.

From the fifty thousand foot level, you are never down and out, you are just stuck for a while, that is all.

Help Others

In our previous lives we have racked up demerits, through our selfish acts, now when we have the chance, we should pay back, using the installment plan to the fullest extent possible. Giving of ourselves is a charitable and worthy act, one that trains our minds to continue on, to never stop being fraternal.

There are two times in most people's lives when they tend to forget others and concentrate on themselves. When times are hard and when times are good. It's human nature.

In between we have the time to consider more than just ourselves. But what in the world is more satisfying that helping out a friend? To feel that you have made an impact is really all that most of us desire.

When you are down, what better way to force you out of your doldrums than forgetting yourself and pitching in for a greater cause.

When I went through a period of unemployment, at first I stayed at home and sent out resume after resume. Feeling dejected and lost.

Finally I pulled myself together and decided to rejoin the world. First with my family. I begin to walk my daughter to school every day. I talked with the other parents.

Then I volunteered to help with a dinner given by the ninth graders. I organized the kids and kept them moving all night. I channeled Captain Bligh and didn't let them rest for a second.

The teachers came up to me afterwards and said they never had a better dinner. I had thrown myself in doing the best job possible.

My helping others affected my interviews, I was more relaxed, more in control. Soon I had new employment.

When the internet boom of the 1990's occurred and technical people were being paid good money for consulting, I made more than I had ever in my life.

What did I do? I worked extra to make more. Did I take time and try to help others, no I planned what new toys I wanted to buy. I went on short expensive vacations, because I was driven to work as many hours as possible.

Do I have any of that money I toiled so hard still? It was all lost, in foolish investments and perishable goods. The only non-perishable good I truly have is myself. I added nothing to it and I contributed nothing to others.

I had lost years for nothing. Except that I learned. I learned never to get on that road again. No matter what the promised rewards are, to live only to gain, to sacrifice your family, your ability to grow spiritually, completely losing your time so you have nothing left to give is not worth the price.

I came to the realization that I must maintain my balance between materialism and spiritualism. I need to work enough to provide a decent living for my family, but putting all else in a lower priority to make sure everyone has the latest gadget and clothes is not a beneficial lesson for my children or for myself.

In violating the seven tenets, in being selfish and making wrong choices during my trials I stopped advancing. Putting love and fraternity first is now seared into my existence.

I learned a harder lesson when I was successful than when I was out of work. This is how the spirit realm guides us in our college on earth. To become a better spirit we must be trained in different circumstances. The key for us, is to maintain our balance and never lose sight of what is important no matter how low or high we are at any one time.

Give Thanks

I am so thankful for my life. I am full of gratitude for the life lessons that have been provided to me. Realizing that my life was planned for my educational benefit has completely changed my outlook.

When I encounter new hurdles, I wonder what this will teach me. And I think about what I probably did in the past to warrant the lesson. I welcome the chance to do better.

Knowing that I am watched over and gently pushed along gives me comfort to remain calm in any circumstance. Well, most circumstances, following my own advice is not easy.

Spiritism tells us that no test is made so you can't pass. Your victory in every situation is assured as long as you don't fight what is being taught and keep your spiritual side with you at all times. Never desist loving and caring for others and you will surpass all expectations.

Finally, always remember you are loved. A type of love that is waiting for you with open arms when you are finished with this life. This small episode of your immortal existence.

Your Exploration Continues . . .

Learn more about Spiritism in my blog at:
http://www.nwspiritism.com.

To assist you in understanding more about Spiritism, I have written four other books.

- Spiritism 101 – The Third Revelation
- Explore Your Destiny – Since Your Life's Path is (mostly) Predetermined
- The Case for Reincarnation – Your Path to Perfection
- What Really Happens During Near Death Experiences According to Spiritism – 12 NDEs Explained and Explored

Below are the introductions to all books.

Spiritism 101 – The Third Revelation

This short book is written as a review of the central concepts of the Doctrine of Spiritism.

Introduction

Something wonderful has happened. It occurred in the middle of the 1800's and it caught the attention of the world. It grew quickly in popularity, so fast that many in positions of power went on a crusade to stamp it out.

Why? Because it provided answers to questions that we all have been searching for. Questions that have been posed by philosophers since the beginning of time were asked and the results fully described.

Why such fear by the ruling religious classes? Because it explained the purpose for our life without dogma, without having to ask a priest or reverend for forgiveness. No special clothes to wear, no diet restrictions. No requirement for a specialized building or monthly stipends.

Why was it scorned? Because it didn't use the word "sin". It talked of spirits. It told us we could come back as either sex. And when it was asked about marriage, we were told that marriage is between two spirits, not two sexes.

We were told that a marriage should be the union of two spirits for as long as they work together in harmony. If not, then it wasn't the spirit world that stopped people from parting, it was our erroneous human convictions.

The organized Christian religions reacted strongly. They burned books and harassed those that knew and cherished the fact that the Third Revelation had occurred.

Like other messages of love, charity and fraternity before; this one was met with strong opposition. Ideas are hard to stamp out and this one is growing again. The world is re-awakening to Spiritism.

Learn what Spiritism is and how it can positively shape your life and happiness.

Explore Your Destiny – Since Your Life's Path is (mostly) Predetermined

Do you wonder if you have an important call with destiny? That you have been selected for something? A cause of a higher purpose?

Well you have been chosen and the why, when, where and how is the subject of this book.

Your life isn't one of just survival through the daily grind of life. The ups and downs of what you have been through are all for a purpose. Every key experience you have had, every calamity that befell you and each relationship that went south or well are part of your overall story. Each major event in your life has been planned.

Have you felt this could be true? Was there even a hint of recognition that certain events occurred for a purpose? And that you were seemingly on a train headed for some unknown destination and you couldn't get off?

This is because within your deepest thoughts, unconsciously, you recognize that you are part of a greater plan. A plan that has been drawn up with your improvement in mind.

There is an answer to your intuition and questions. The answer is wonderful and your part in the drama you are leading is fascinating. Once you realize the total environment in which you reside in, you will recognize that your life is not dreary, but a heart stopping adventure, a roller coaster ride that drives you forward into an unimaginable future.

Explore Your Destiny is divided into four sections. Each section supplies one more piece of the puzzle for you to place, so you can look at your life's arc with new insights.

1. Why – Why are we here and why must we live what we are living through right now? It's the age old expression, that we all say at one time or another, "Why me?" Well there is a reason and it will be explained to you.

2. When – In what period along your souls timeline is all of this happening? Yes, there is a greater context of your soul, which you may not be aware of. Knowing your relative position in the path to perfection will guide you to understanding your current life.

3. How – How does all of this occur? How does the entire process affect your destiny and actions? What are the rules of the game? Knowing the structure and comprehending the basic laws that direct your life provides you with a point of view that will put everything into perspective.

4. Where – Where is this world that plans our destiny? Are there good places to be and are there bad? Where does the earth fit into the logical structure? You will see where the regions that you are striving to attain are and

where you may be living in your not-to-distant future.

I hope that after reading this book you will have a new view of your life. A view that allows you to look at your circumstances from afar and identify the turning points in your personal destiny. I want you to be in that high level observation tower where you can dispassionately evaluate your life and calmly proceed through the good and bad times. Always keeping your eye on the ball of what your true goal really is – Your triumph in the Spirit and Physical worlds.

My book is available at Amazon; *Explore Your Destiny – Since Your Life's Path is (mostly) Predetermined.*

The Case for Reincarnation – Your Path to Perfection

To fully understand the emotions of the people living through their NDEs and the actions of the spirit world in sending people back to earth, a review of how and why we travel through multiple lives is helpful.

You have lived multiple lives. At times you have been rich, poor, a servant and a slave. Maybe even a King or a Queen, at the least a member of the minor nobility.

Many famous people in the past have believed in reincarnation, such as Thomas Edison and Sir Arthur Conan Doyle. They both believed in the spirit world and made attempts to communicate with the world beyond.

There is a realm, a universe greater than ours and it is filled with intelligences that we can only wonder at. There are spirits around the earth who are actively helping and guiding us in our planning and during our actual incarnations.

You are interested in this book and in the topic because you know, in your heart that we are not merely chemical elements that dissolve with death. There must be something more, you know this, because of your own intuition, experiences and beliefs.

There are too many unexplained phenomena for there to be nothing after death. How do some people have past life memories? Why do children remember past lives and then lose the ability after a certain age? How can some people know the future? And more importantly, why do you have premonitions that come true? How could you know what could happen with such certainty?

Reincarnation is a tenet in many religions, such as Hinduism and Buddhism, and is frequently mentioned as parts of varied sects of Christianity and Judaism. It is the concept whereby we have a spirit, in which we retain our central personalities and memories, while in the spirit world, but lose our memories while in a physical form.

This book is here to answer your questions;

1. Why do we reincarnate?
2. How does the process work?
3. How many reincarnations must we have?
4. What memories do we retain from our previous lives?
5. Do we have control over our reincarnations?
6. Why must we suffer?
7. How may I insure my next life is better?
8. How may I progress to being a perfected spirit?

These questions are answered through the Doctrine of Spiritism. When, in the 1850's, the spirit world determine it was time for the human race to assimilate this knowledge in the hopes it would led us to understand the need to improve our spirituality and to achieve a better balance between our desire for material goods versus our desire to be a better person.

Explore what is your role and where you are in this journey. Determine your place and your future. Find out the reasons for your current tribulations and how to, not only survive your trials, but prosper through them.

Your journey in different bodies at different times in different circumstances is not without a purpose. You began as a primitive soul and through successive lives; you are being molded into a perfect spirit.

Dive deeper into all facets of reincarnation; my book is available at Amazon; *The Case for Reincarnation – Your Path to Perfection*

What Really Happens During Near Death Experiences, According to Spiritism

12 NDE's Explained and Explored

Why are we interested in Near Death Experiences (NDE)? With the advent of the internet, social media allows masses of people to more efficiently pool together shared experiences than at any other time in history. What was once an isolated phenomenon is now a common occurrence. Whereas, in times past a simple farmer or a rich landowner who would be able to pull back from death, their story, if they chose to tell it, would be a solitary happenstance. Easily explained away or believed. It made no difference, since the significance of the account would be eventually dismissed as an outlying data point.

The recent improvement in the speed and efficiency of human

communication in conjunction with modern medical methods of assisting the human body to recover after trauma has supported the explosion of accounts. And as the interpretations of each individual who returned became widely known and disseminated, others choose to finally reveal their own personal story.

Therefore a small bookshelf of NDEs is now becoming a library. Recollections from every country, culture, language and age group now reside in the great internet cloud. A mountain of data, which can no longer be wished away or ignored. The parallels and common themes from all corners of the world preclude everyone's account to be merely mass hysteria. NDEs aren't in the territory of alien encounters. Doctors, lawyers, professors, engineers, sales and service people are reporting in. Telling us similar refrains, with the added mystery of some NDEs where the person either saw or is told of events that they could not have possibly known in their current state. Taken as a whole, the only conclusion is that something must be happening, beyond our comprehension.

My book is available at Amazon: *What Really Happens During Near Death Experiences – 12 NDEs Explained and Explored is available at Amazon.*

Author

Stay in touch with the author via:

Spiritist Blog: http://www.nwspiritism.com

Facebook: https://www.facebook.com/nwspiritism

Facebook group to discuss Spiritism: (please request to join)
https://www.facebook.com/groups/Spiritist/

Twitter: https://twitter.com/nwspiritism

If you liked *7 Tenets of Spiritism – How They Impact Your Daily Life*, please post a review at Amazon.

Copyright

Version 2015.05.15.02

Bibliography

Denis, L. (2012). *Life and Destiny.* Forgotten Books.

Kardec, A. (2006). *Heaven and Hell.* Brasilia (DF), Brasil: International Spiritist Council.

Kardec, A. (2008). *The Gospel According to Spiritism.* Brasilia (DF): International Spiritist Council.

Kardec, A. (2009). *Genesis - Miracles and Predictions according to Spiritism.* Brasilia (DF), Brasil: International Spiritist Council.

Kardec, A. (2010). *The Spirits Book.* Guildford, UK: White Crow Books.

Swedenborg, E. (1758). *Heaven and Hell.* Europe: A Publice Domain Book.

Wikipedia. (2014, August 21). *Camilo Castelo Branco.* Retrieved from Wikipedia: http://en.wikipedia.org/wiki/Camilo_Castelo_Branco

Xavier, F. C. (2004). *In the Domain of Mediumship.* New York: Spiritist Alliance of Books, Inc.

Xavier, F. C. (2008). *The Messengers.* Philadelphia, PA: Allan Kardec Educational Society.

Xavier, F. C. (2008). *Workers of the Life Eternal.* Brasilia (DF) - Brazil: International Spiritist Council.

Xavier, F. C. (2009). *And Life Goes On.* Brasilia (DF), Brasil: International Spiritist Council.

Xavier, F. C. (2009). *In the Greater World.* Brasilia (DF), Brazil: International Spiritist Council.

Xavier, F. C. (2009). *Missionaries of the Light.* Brasilia (DF), Brazil: International Spiritist Council.

Xavier, F. C. (2010). *Action and Reaction.* Brasilia (DF), Brazil: International Spiritist Council.

Xavier, F. C. (2010). *Nosso Lar.* Brasilia - (DF), Brazil: International Spiritist Council.

Xavier, F. C. (2011). *Between Heaven and Earth.* Brasilia (DF), Brazil: International Spiritist Council.

Xavier, F. C. (2011). *In the Realms of Mediumship.* Brasilia (DF), Brazil: EDICEI.

Xavier, F. C. (2011). *On the Way to the Light.* Brasilia (DF), Brazil: International Spiritist Council.

Xavier, F. C. (2013). *Liberation.* Brasilia (DF), Brazil: International Spiritist Council.

Xavier, F. C. (2013). *Sex and Destiny.* Miami, FL: EDICEI of America.

[1] Wikipedia, "Chico Xavier", n.d., http://en.wikipedia.org/wiki/Chico_Xavier, (accessed May 4, 2014)
[2] Wikipedia, "Chico Xavier", n.d., http://en.wikipedia.org/wiki/Chico_Xavier, (accessed May 4, 2014)
[3] Neto, G. L. Remembering Chico Xavier and His Legacy, YouTube, (accessed May 3, 2014)
[4] Xavier, Francisco C. In the Greater World, EDICEI, p. 158
[5] Xavier, Francisco C. In the Greater World, EDICEI, p. 158
[6] Xavier, Francisco C. In the Greater World, EDICEI, p. 158
[7] Xavier, Francisco C. In the Greater World, EDICEI, p. 159
[8] Hooper, Richard, Jesus, Buddha, Krishna & Lao Tzu, Bristol Park Books, pp. 138-139
[9] Pereira, Y. A., Memoirs of a Suicide, EDICEI, p. 528
[10] Pereira, Y. A., Memoirs of a Suicide, EDICEI, p. 529
[11] Xavier, F.C. Missionaries of the Light, EDICEI, pp. 154-155

CPSIA information can be obtained
at www.ICGtesting.com
Printed in the USA
FSOW04n1251030417
32664FS